GRAMMAR
FOR GREAT WRITING

A

SERIES CONSULTANT:
KEITH S. FOLSE

LAURIE BLASS

KEITH S. FOLSE

DEBORAH A. MITCHELL

NATIONAL GEOGRAPHIC LEARNING

CENGAGE Learning

Australia • Brazil • Mexico • Singapore • United Kingdom • United States

Grammar for Great Writing:
Student Book A, **First Edition**
Laurie Blass • Keith S. Folse
• Deborah A. Mitchell

Publisher: Sherrise Roehr

Executive Editor: Laura Le Dréan

Senior Development Editor: Jennifer Bixby

Media Researcher: Leila Hishmeh

Senior Technology Product Manager: Scott Rule

Director of Global Marketing: Ian Martin

Product Marketing Manager: Dalia Bravo

Sr. Director, ELT & World Languages: Michael Burggren

Production Manager: Daisy Sosa

Content Project Manager: Beth Houston

Senior Print Buyer: Mary Beth Hennebury

Composition: SPi-Global

Cover/Text Design: Brenda Carmichael

Art Director: Brenda Carmichael

Cover Image: Keith Ladzinski ©Keith Ladzinski/ Aurora Photos; Sunrise on the crest of frost-covered sand dunes in Great Sand Dunes National Park, Colorado.

For product information and technology assistance, contact us at
Cengage Learning Customer & Sales Support, cengage.com/contact

For permission to use material from this text or product,
submit all requests online at **cengage.com/permissions**
Further permissions questions can be emailed to
permissionrequest@cengage.com

Student Edition:
ISBN: 978-1-337-11583-4

National Geographic Learning
20 Channel Center Street
Boston, MA 02210
USA

National Geographic Learning, a Cengage Learning Company, has a mission to bring the world to the classroom and the classroom to life. With our English language programs, students learn about their world by experiencing it. Through our partnerships with National Geographic and TED, they develop the language and skills they need to be successful global citizens and leaders.

Locate your local office at **international.cengage.com/region**

Visit National Geographic Learning online at **NGL.cengage.com/ELT**
Visit our corporate website at **www.cengage.com**

Printed in the United States of America
Print Number: 01 Print Year: 2016

Contents

Scope and Sequence

Unit	Common Errors	Vocabulary in Academic Writing	Kinds of Writing
1 **Using *Be* in Sentences**	1.1 Does the verb agree with the subject? 1.2 Is your sentence complete? 1.3 Do you need *be* or *have*?	*Adjectives Frequently Used with* Be available important similar consistent likely useful different necessary willing essential	Descriptive: *The Republic of Maldives* Definition: *Plagiarism*
2 **Using *Have* in Sentences**	2.1 Does the verb agree with the subject? 2.2 Do you need *have* or *be*?	*Nouns Frequently Used with* Have access difficulty opportunity benefits effect right consequences meaning time control	Comparison: *The Japanese and American Systems of Government* Comparison: *Bees and Wasps*
3 **Writing with the Simple Present**	3.1 Do the subject and the verb agree? 3.2 Is the verb *be* missing? 3.3 Is the adverb in the correct position?	*Adverbs + Verbs Frequently Used in the Present* always seem often find sometimes make always take often use usually mean never get sometimes feel usually occur never know	Cause–Effect: *The Keys to Happiness* Opinion: *Digital Books vs. Printed Books*
4 **Writing with the Present Progressive**	4.1 Is the present progressive form correct? 4.2 Is the spelling correct? 4.3 Do you need simple present or present progressive? 4.4 Is it a stative verb?	*Verbs Frequently Used in Present Progressive* become make use begin take work do try	Descriptive: *Bike-Friendly Cities* Cause–Effect: *Changes in the American Diet*
5 **Writing with the Simple Past**	5.1 Do you need simple present or simple past? 5.2 Do you use the correct form? 5.3 Are your verb tenses consistent? 5.4 Is the negative form correct?	*Verbs Frequently Used in Simple Past* associate have provide base include report be make say do	Narrative (Biography): *Ibn Battuta, World Traveler* Narrative (Biography): *Marie Curie*
6 **Writing with the Past Progressive**	6.1 Do you have the correct past progressive form? 6.2 Do you need simple past or past progressive?	*Verbs Frequently Used with* While *in the Past Progressive* attend read try do take use learn teach work make	Narrative (Biography): *Marianna Yampolsky* Narrative: *The First and Last Trip of the Titanic*
7 **Writing about the Future**	7.1 Do you have the correct form with *will* or *may*? 7.2 Do you have the correct future form?	*Verbs Frequently Used with* May be include provide find lead result have need seem help	Descriptive: *Doctors' Appointments in the Future* Cause–Effect: *The Dangers of Plastic Garbage in the Oceans*
8 **Writing with Subject–Verb Agreement**	8.1 Is the verb form correct? 8.2 Does the verb agree with the subject?	*Verbs from the Academic Word List (Sublist 1)* assume function occur create indicate require distribute involve vary estimate	Descriptive: *The Amazing Jindo-Modo Land Bridge* Descriptive: *Animal Communication*

Unit	Common Errors	Vocabulary in Academic Writing	Kinds of Writing
9 **Writing with Prepositions and Prepositional Phrases**	9.1 Do you have the correct preposition? 9.2 Do you have a gerund after a preposition? 9.3 Is there an error with *for*?	*Frequently Used Adjective + Preposition Combinations* aware of ⸻ involved in concerned about ⸻ related to different from ⸻ responsible for interested in ⸻ similar to	Narrative (Biography): *Steve Jobs* Narrative (Biography): *William Shakespeare*
10 **Writing with Modals**	10.1 Is the form of the modal correct? 10.2 Do you need a modal? 10.3 Is it the correct modal?	*Verbs Frequently Used with* Can be ⸻ lead ⸻ see do ⸻ make ⸻ take have ⸻ provide ⸻ use help	Process: *How to Start a Community Garden* Cause–Effect: *Dangers of Medicines for Babies*
11 **Using Simple Sentences**	11.1 Is there a complete verb form? 11.2 Is there a subject? 11.3 Do you have the correct punctuation for items in a series? 11.4 Is there a comma after an introductory phrase?	*Words from the Academic Word List (Sublist 2)* affect ⸻ focus categories ⸻ previous complex ⸻ primary consequences ⸻ region design ⸻ strategies	Descriptive: *The Valuable and Spicy Chili Pepper* Descriptive: *Results of Commuting Survey*
12 **Using Compound Sentences**	12.1 Is there a coordinating conjunction? 12.2 Is a comma missing? 12.3 Can you use a compound sentence? 12.4 Does the sentence begin with a coordinating conjunction?	*Words from the Academic Word List (Sublist 3)* document ⸻ negative ⸻ sequence initial ⸻ outcomes ⸻ sufficient instance ⸻ removed ⸻ task location	Descriptive: *The Science Behind a Roller Coaster* Descriptive: *The FIFA World Cup*
13 **Writing with Adjectives**	13.1 Is the adjective in the correct position? 13.2 Is the adjective correct? 13.3 Is the comparative form correct?	*Frequently Used Adjectives* different ⸻ new ⸻ public high ⸻ other ⸻ significant important ⸻ political ⸻ social international	Narrative (Science Report): *The Effect of Sunlight on Plant Growth* Comparison: *Alligators and Crocodiles*
14 **Writing with Articles**	14.1 Do you use *a/an/the* correctly? 14.2 Do you use *a/an* with a non-count noun? 14.3 Do you need *the*?	*Nouns Frequently Used with* An attempt ⸻ explanation ⸻ object effort ⸻ increase ⸻ opportunity element ⸻ instrument ⸻ overview examination	Descriptive: *Pearls* Definition: *Farming for Fish*
15 **Writing with Adverbs**	15.1 Do you use the adverb form of the word? 15.2 Is the adverb of manner in the correct position? 15.3 Is the frequency adverb in the correct position? 15.4 Is the adverb of degree correct and in the correct position?	*Adverbs Frequently Used with* Very carefully ⸻ likely ⸻ recently clearly ⸻ often ⸻ slowly closely ⸻ quickly ⸻ well far	Opinion: *Kevin Durant: A True Sportsman* Process: *Collecting Water from Air*

Overview

ABOUT THE *GRAMMAR FOR GREAT WRITING* SERIES

Grammar for Great Writing is a three-book series that helps students with the specific grammar they actually need to strengthen their academic writing. Activities feature academic vocabulary and content, providing clear models for good academic writing. Ideal for the grammar component of a writing and grammar class, *Grammar for Great Writing* may be used as a companion to the *Great Writing* series or in conjunction with any academic writing textbook.

This series consists of three levels: A, B, and C.

Book A is for low intermediate students and is designed to complement the writing and grammar found in *Great Writing 2*.

Book B is for intermediate students and is designed to complement the writing and grammar found in *Great Writing 3*.

Book C is for upper intermediate to advanced students and is designed to complement the writing and grammar found in *Great Writing 4*.

ORGANIZATION

Each of the three books in this series consists of 15 units, and each unit focuses solidly on one area of grammar that causes problems for ESL and EFL writers. These 45 grammar points have been selected based on input from experienced English language teachers and student writers. Although many grammar points appear in only one book, others are so important that they appear in more than one book. Students work with the grammar point in increasingly more complex sentences and rhetorical modes as they progress through the different levels of the series.

The units have been carefully designed so that they may be taught in any order. In fact, it is possible to skip units if teachers believe that a particular grammar point is not problematic for their students. In other words, teachers should review the table of contents, which calls out the common student errors addressed in each unit, and carefully choose which of the 15 grammar topics to present and in which order.

CONTENTS OF A UNIT

Each of the six sections in a unit contains presentation and practice. Although each unit has a specific grammatical focus, the following sections appear in every unit:

What Do You Know?

This opening activity is designed to grab the students' attention and help them assess their understanding of the grammar point. *What Do You Know* has two parts. First students are directed to look at the unit opening photo and think about how it is related to the topic of the paragraph. They discuss two questions related to the photo that are designed to elicit use of the target grammar. Then students read the paragraph that has two common errors in it. The paragraph has a clear rhetorical style. Students work together to find the grammar errors and explain the corrections.

Grammar Forms

Clear charts present and explain the form of the unit's grammar focus. Follow-up activities focus students' attention on the grammar form.

Common Uses

How the grammar is used in writing is a unique part of the series. The common use charts explain how the grammar point is actually used in academic writing. A follow-up activity provides practice.

Common Errors

Here students are presented with a series of two to five of the most common errors that student writers typically make with the unit grammar point. The focus is on errors found in academic writing, and each error chart is followed by an activity.

Academic Vocabulary

Academic vocabulary is a unique feature of this series. Using corpus and frequency data, we have identified vocabulary that most naturally combines with the grammar focus of the unit. The *Vocabulary in Academic Writing* activity presents items from a broad range of academic subject areas.

Put It Together

The *Review Quiz* gives teachers a chance to quickly check how much students have learned about forming and using the grammar point. In this short activity of only eight items, students answer five multiple-choice questions and then identify and correct errors in three items.

In *Building Greater Sentences,* students combine three or more short sentences into one coherent sentence that uses the target grammar structure.

Steps to Composing is an engaging and interactive activity in which students read a paragraph consisting of 8 to 12 sentences. The paragraph models a specific rhetorical style. While none of the sentences contain outright errors, the writing can be improved. To this end, there are 10 steps that instruct the student in how to improve the sentences. Most of the time the instructions are very specific (for example, combine sentences 2 and 3 with the word *because*). Other times they are intentionally more open in order to challenge the student (for example, add a descriptive adjective to the sentence).

Finally, *Original Writing* consists of a writing assignment connected to the grammar topic, focusing on a specific rhetorical style of writing. There are three example sentences to give the student ideas for a topic. The amount of writing that is required will depend on the student, the teacher, and the objectives for the course.

Acknowledgements

I am grateful to the many people who have worked so hard on the development and production of *Grammar for Great Writing*, including Laura Le Dréan and Jennifer Bixby of National Geographic Learning, and authors Laurie Blass and Deborah Mitchell. Ultimately, everyone's ideas and feedback have been instrumental in the design of this work.

Grammar for Great Writing is the result of many years of teaching academic writing to students all over the world. Therefore, I would also like to acknowledge the input from the thousands of ESL and EFL students that I have taught throughout my teaching career. This series is very much based on learner needs, particularly grammar problems that I have seen students struggle with as they are trying to improve their academic writing in English. These classroom experiences have been instrumental in shaping which grammar is covered as well as how it is presented and practiced.

Finally, many thanks to the following reviewers who offered important ideas and helpful suggestions that shaped the *Grammar for Great Writing* series:

Nancy Boyer, Golden West College, California

Tony Carnerie, University of California, San Diego Language Institute, California

Angela Cox, Spring International Language Center, Arkansas

Luke Daly, Harold Washington College, Illinois

Rachel Dictor, DePaul University English Language Academy, Illinois

Ian Dreilinger, Center for Multilingual Multicultural Studies, Florida

Edward Feighny, Houston Community College, Texas

Timothy Fojtik, Concordia University Wisconsin, Wisconsin

Janile Hill, DePaul University English Language Academy, Illinois

Elizabeth Kelley, University of California, San Diego Language Institute, California

Toby Killcreas, Auburn University at Montgomery, Alabama

Lisa Kovacs, University of California, San Diego Language Institute, California

Maria Lerma, Orange Coast College, California

Wendy McBride, University of Arkansas, Spring International Language Center, Arkansas

Kathy Najafi, Houston Community College, Texas

Anne Politz, Drexel University, Pennsylvania

Wendy Ramer, Broward Community College, Florida

Helen Roland, Miami Dade College, Florida

Kody Salzburn, Auburn University at Montgomery, Alabama

Gail Schwartz, University of California, Irvine, California

Karen Shock, Savannah College of Art and Design, Georgia

Adriana Treadway, Spring International Language Center, Arkansas

Anne McGee Tyoan, Savannah College of Art and Design, Georgia

—Keith S. Folse

Series Consultant

Photo Credits

Cover: Keith Ladzinski/Aurora Photos.

02–03 Franco Banfi/Nature Picture Library, **05** (b) Qi Yang/Moment/Getty Images, **13** (t) Doug Lemke/Shutterstock.com, **16–17** Haru Miura/EyeEm/Getty Images, **25** (t) Images by Dr. Alan Lipkin/Shutterstock.com, **28–29** Nicky Loh/Reuters, **38** (t) The Sydney Morning Herald/Getty Images, **40–41** Lalo de Almeida/The New York Times/Redux, **51** (t) Thierlein/ullstein bild/Getty Images, **54–55** Bibliotheque Nationale de France/National Geographic Creative, **57** (b) Omar Havana/Getty Images, **65** (t) Andrea Danti/Shutterstock.com, **68–69** Heriberto Rodriguez, **72** (br) Science Photo Library/Superstock, **77** (t) GORAN EHLME/National Geographic Creative, **80–81** Jean Francois Monier/AFP/Getty Images, **86** (b) Tom Merton/Caiaimage/Getty Images, **89** (t) Tom Reichner/Shutterstock.com, **92–93** Martin Bennie/500px Prime, **95** (b) LYNN JOHNSON/National Geographic Creative, **99** (b) peisen zhao/E+/Getty Images, **103** (t) Richard Packwood/Getty Images, **106–107** Michael L. Abramson/Getty Images, **117** (t) ANNIE GRIFFITHS/National Geographic Creative, **120–121** Matt Cardy/Getty Images News/Getty Images, **123** (b) Colin Anderson/Blend Images/Getty Images, **131** (t) Tan Yilmaz/Getty Images, **134–135** Paul Harris/JWL/Aurora Photos, **142** (b) Clarissa Leahy/Getty Images, **145** (t) Minerva Studio/Shutterstock.com, **148–149** KAZUHIRO NOGI/AFP/Getty Images, **151** (b) Aeypix/Shutterstock.com, **159** (t) bierchen/Shutterstock.com, **162–163** Jim Richardson/National Geographic Creative, **167** (b) Paolo Gallo/Shutterstock.com, **173** (t) George Rose/Getty Images, **176–177** Jon Hicks/Getty Images, **184** (b) On SET/Shutterstock.com, **187** (t) GUDKOV ANDREY/Shutterstock.com, **190–191** Jim McIsaac/Getty Images, **193** (b) DESIGN PICS INC/National Geographic Creative, **203** (t) MICHAEL NICHOLS/National Geographic Creative.

References

Coxhead, A. (2000). See http://www.victoria.ac.nz/lals/resources/academicwordlist/

Davies, M. (2008–). *The corpus of contemporary American English: 520 million words, 1990–present.* See http://corpus.byu.edu/coca/

Coral reefs under shallow waters near the Maldives islands are home to many kinds of fish.

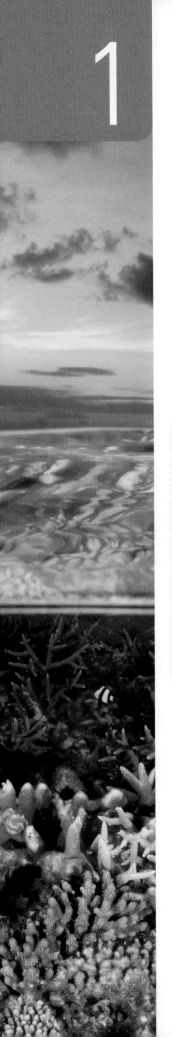

1 Using *Be* in Sentences

WHAT DO YOU KNOW?

DISCUSS Look at the photo and read the caption. Discuss the questions.

1. These coral reefs are in the Indian Ocean. Where else can you find coral reefs?

2. What lives in a coral reef?

FIND THE ERRORS This paragraph contains two errors with the verb *be*. Find the errors and correct them. Explain your corrections to a partner.

DESCRIPTIVE PARAGRAPH

The Republic of Maldives

¹ The Republic of Maldives is an island nation in the Indian Ocean. ² The country is actually a group of over a thousand small islands. ³ Most of these islands are only about 5 feet (1.5 meters) above sea level. ⁴ In fact, the Republic of Maldives the lowest country in the world. ⁵ Tourism and fishing is the main sources of income for the country. ⁶ Over a million tourists visit the Maldives each year. ⁷ They come to enjoy the warm weather and the beautiful white beaches. ⁸ The islands are also famous for their coral reefs. ⁹ The reefs are home to sea turtles, whales, dolphins, and over 1,100 species of fish.

Grammar Forms

1.1 Simple Present: *Be*

Subject	Verb	Example
I	*am*	I speak English and Chinese, so I **am** bilingual.
he / she / it	*is*	Global warming **is** a problem for small island nations.
you / we / they	*are*	The benefits of daily exercise **are** enormous.

Notes
1. To form the negative, put *not* after a form of *be*.

    Koalas **are not** active during the daytime.
2. A gerund is a singular subject.

    Playing computer games **is** a popular hobby.
3. Contractions are almost never used in academic writing.

1.2 Simple Past: *Be*

Subject	Verb	Example
I / he / she / it	*was*	Kyoto **was** the capital of Japan until 1889.
you / we / they	*were*	In the past, polio and smallpox **were** serious diseases in the United States.

1.3 Simple Present: *There + Be*

In sentences with *there + be*, the subject comes after the verb. The verb agrees with the subject.

There + Be	Example
There is + singular subject	**There is** evidence that children and adults do not hear music in the same way.
There are + plural subject	**There are** several important differences between whales and dolphins.

1.4 Simple Past: *There + Be*

Verb	Example
There was + singular subject	**There was** more <u>interest</u> in studying history in the early 1900s.
There were + plural subject	In 1491, **there were** over 100 million <u>Native Americans</u> in the New World, according to some historians.

Note
In academic writing, it is more common to use *there + be + no* in the negative form.

> **There was no** doubt that Kain's hypothesis was correct.

1.5 *Be* + Adjective + Infinitive

It + Be	Adjective + Infinitive	Example
It is	*important / useful / difficult / likely* + infinitive	**It is important to understand** the causes of global warming.

ACTIVITY 1

Fill in the blank with the correct form of *be*.

1. For some people, it _____ difficult to learn a second language.

2. There _____ three main causes of rain.

3. Nguyen Van Thieu _____ the president of South Vietnam from 1967 to 1975.

4. The results of the experiment are unclear, so there _____ a need for more study.

5. Farming and home building _____ the greatest dangers for wild animals that live nearby.

6. In 1972, there _____ only one American hamburger restaurant in France, but now there are thousands.

7. Modern-day Croatia and the Czech Republic _____ both part of the Austro-Hungarian Empire until 1918.

8. In my opinion, the class was too large for effective learning because there _____ over 50 students.

Common Uses

1.6 Using *Be*

The verb *be* is very common in writing. *Be* is used:

1. to define the subject or give more information about it	The black mamba **is** the world's longest snake. The black mamba snake **is not** actually black in color.
2. to describe the subject with adjectives	Lions, tigers, and other big cats **are** dangerous. Lions **are not** the largest of the big cats.
3. to describe the location of the subject (with a preposition)	The new marine park **is** in the African nation of Gabon. The Cape Verde Islands **are not** in the Indian Ocean.
4. to present an opinion (*it* + *be* + adjective + infinitve)	It **is** important to practice a new language every day. For many people, it **is not** easy to save money.

Note

Be is used to describe a person or thing, or to describe a location. Use *have* to indicate ownership, relationships, or parts of a whole. (See Unit 2, Using *Have* in Sentences.)

Cameron County **is** in southeastern Texas.
Texas **has** 254 counties.

1.7 Using *There + Be*

There + be is used in writing:

1. to write about categories or types of something	**There are** two types of camels: the dromedary and the Bactrian. **There are** over 4,000 varieties of native potatoes in Peru, Bolivia, and Ecuador.
2. to say that something exists or existed	**There are** 100 participants in the study. **There were no** libraries in this area before 1991.

Fill in the blank with the correct form of *be*. Use *no* or *not* when it is there.

1. There _____ over 7 billion people living on Earth today.

2. According to the World Database of Happiness, Switzerland _____ the world's happiest nation in 2015.

3. Biofuels _____ fuels that come from plants.

4. There _____ (*no*) California condors in the wild between 1988 and 1991.

5. Contrary to what many people think, there _____ (*no*) earthquake season.

6. Some research suggests that walking _____ better for weight loss than running.

7. One of the main causes of sleep problems _____ stress.

8. The Shanghai Tower _____ (*not*) as tall as the Burj Khalifa.

The Shanghai Tower in Pudong, China, is 2,073 feet (632 meters) tall.

Common Errors

Common Error 1.1 Does the verb agree with the subject?

are
<u>Both</u> English and French ~~is~~ official languages in Canada.

are
<u>There</u> ~~is~~ three <u>types</u> of volcanoes.

is
<u>One</u> of the best areas to see wildlife ~~are~~ East Africa.

was
<u>Offering</u> more scholarships ~~were~~ a top priority last year.

REMEMBER: • Use the correct singular or plural verb form. *Both* takes a plural verb.
- In sentences with *there*, the subject always follows the verb.
- Identify the subject by looking for the main noun or pronoun.
- Gerund subjects are singular.

ACTIVITY 3 Common Error 1.1

Underline the correct form of the verb in the parentheses.

1. There (*is / are*) five types of computers: laptops, desktops, servers, mainframes, and supercomputers.

2. Some research suggests that drinking bottled water (*is / are*) bad for your health.

3. The production of meat (*is / are*) one of the main contributors to climate change.

4. In the year 1800, the world population (*was / were*) 1 billion.

5. Mining and farming (*is / are*) two of the main causes of water pollution.

6. One responsibility of a chief executive officer (CEO) (*is / are*) to develop the company's long-term plan.

7. At 116 years old, Susannah Mushatt Jones (*was / were*) the world's oldest living person in 2015.

8. There (*was / were*) over 7.5 million cars in the United States by 1920.

ACTIVITY 4 Common Error 1.1

In each paragraph, fill in the blank with the correct form of *be*.

1. Overfishing _____ catching so many fish that they cannot replace themselves. Overfishing means we have fewer fish to eat. It _____ also harmful to other plants and animals in the ocean.

2. There _____ three techniques for improving memory. One way _____ to stop using your GPS for directions and to use your memory instead. For example, if you _____ a visual person, study a route map and memorize it. If you _____ a verbal person, memorize the directions as a list of steps.

3. The poison dart frog _____ a small frog that lives in Central America. These frogs _____ very colorful. They can be yellow, orange, or light green. There _____ more than 100 different types of poison dart frogs.

4. When I _____ a child, Belleville _____ a quiet, sleepy town. It _____ difficult to find a job in Belleville in those days. In fact, everyone worked in the nearby city, and they took the train to get there. As a result, there _____ very little traffic in Belleville. Today, however, traffic _____ a big problem in my hometown.

Common Error 1.2 Is your sentence complete?

When Barack Obama became president in 2009, *he* was 47 years old.

Global warming *is* a threat to island nations.

Because of the drought, *there* were many serious consequences for local farmers.

REMEMBER: • Use subject + *be*.
• Use *there* + *be* when you say something exists.

ACTIVITY 5   Common Error 1.2

Read each sentence. Find the missing words. Write a caret (^) where the missing word should be. Then write the correct word above the caret.

1. The lion is one of the fastest mammals in the world, but it not as fast as the cheetah.

2. Are three main types of rocks: sedimentary, metamorphic, and igneous.

3. The inland taipan is one of the world's most poisonous snakes, but is not the most dangerous.

4. Over 10 thousand years ago, were trees, plants, and plenty of water in the Sahara Desert.

5. Until 1997, Almaty was the capital of Kazakhstan, but now is Astana.

6. In the past, were billions of passenger pigeons on Earth, but the very last one, Martha, died in a zoo over 100 years ago.

7. In the future, is likely that humans will live on Mars.

8. The Empire State Building was the tallest building in the world, but now there many taller buildings.

Common Error 1.3 Do you need *be* or *have*?

is
Singapore ~~has~~ an island city-state.

are
There ~~have~~ four official languages in Singapore.

REMEMBER:
- Use *be* to identify someone or something and to describe location.
- Use *have* to indicate possession or ownership, relationships, or parts of a whole.
- Use *there + be* to state that something or someone exists, or that something is a fact. The most common verb with *there* is *be*.

ACTIVITY 6 Common Error 1.3

Underline the correct verb.

1. Many household cleaning products (*have / are*) harmful to humans.

2. When a camel (*has / is*) really thirsty, it can drink up to 30 gallons (135 liters) of water in about 13 minutes.

3. There (*have / are*) many reasons why it is important to have a college degree.

4. The Singapore Zoo (*has / is*) over 300 species of mammals, birds, and reptiles.

5. Taipei 101 (*had / was*) the world's tallest building until 2010.

6. Kenya, for example, (*has / is*) a limited supply of fresh water.

7. Singapore (*has / is*) four official languages: Malay, Mandarin, Tamil, and English.

8. Elephants (*have / are*) the largest land animals on Earth.

Academic Vocabulary

Adjectives Frequently Used with *Be* in Academic Writing

available	different	important	necessary	useful
consistent	essential	likely	similar	willing

Source: Corpus of Contemporary American English (Davies 2008–)

ACTIVITY 7 **Vocabulary in Academic Writing**

Use the correct form of *be* to fill in the blanks and underline the correct academic vocabulary to complete the sentences. Use *not* when it is there.

Subject Area	Example from Academic Writing
Education	**1.** A large library _____ (*different / necessary*) to help children become better readers.
Environmental Science	**2.** In this country, earthquakes _____ more (*likely / willing*) to occur on the coast than in the inland areas.
English Composition	**3.** First of all, hybrid cars _____ (*different / willing*) from electric cars in terms of cost.
Business	**4.** Finally, training in the workplace _____ (*similar / important*) in that it helps workers learn skills they can use on the job.
Psychology	**5.** We still do not know how birth order affects personality, so more research on this issue _____ (*essential / available*).
Urban Design	**6.** Communities are healthier when recreation areas _____ (*willing / available*) to residents.
Economics	**7.** The cost of living _____ (*not*) always (*consistent / important*) with the amount of money people can earn.
Sociology	**8.** Hobbes and Malthus _____ (*similar / available*) in their ideas on what motivates people.
English Composition	**9.** Although a computer science degree may _____ (*willing / useful*) in getting a job, it does not lead to a complete understanding of computer science.
Literature	**10.** The story's hero _____ (*willing / consistent*) to give up something of value—for example, his own life—in order to achieve a goal.

Put It Together

Review Quiz

Multiple Choice   Choose the letter of the correct answer.

1. Soil _____ four components: rocks, water, air, and leaves.

   a. is   **b.** have   **c.** has   **d.** are

2. There _____ several reasons why I am learning English.

   a. is   **b.** was   **c.** have   **d.** are

3. One of the most important aspects of employee satisfaction _____ a sense of control over the work environment.

   a. is   **b.** are   **c.** have   **d.** has

4. In that year, the total rainfall in California _____ only 49 percent of the historical average.

   a. were   **b.** was   **c.** is   **d.** are

5. Before cable television became common, there _____ only four television stations in most parts of the country. Now there are hundreds.

   a. is   **b.** are   **c.** were   **d.** was

Error Correction   One of the five underlined words or phrases is not correct. Find the error and correct it. Be prepared to explain your answer.

6. There <u>are</u> many <u>reason</u> for <u>studying</u> a second language, such as enjoying travel more and being able to <u>work</u> in a <u>foreign</u> country.

7. Steinstra's main point <u>are</u> that social media <u>is</u> useful <u>for</u> helping people to <u>practice</u> relationship management techniques <u>in</u> a low-stress environment.

8. <u>In 2013</u>, <u>were</u> 30 million Internet users <u>in</u> Pakistan. <u>Over 15 million</u> of these people used mobile <u>devices</u> to connect to the Internet.

Sunrise colors the mountains in Death Valley National Park in California.

Building Greater Sentences

Combine these short sentences into one sentence. You can add new words and move words around, but you should not add or omit any ideas. More than one answer is possible, but all of these sentences require the verb *be*. (See Appendix 1, Building Greater Sentences, page 206, for tips on how to do this activity.)

1. **a.** Death Valley is one of the hottest places on Earth.
   b. This is because it is located below sea level.
   c. This is because it is far from any sources of water.

   _____

   _____

2. **a.** Cats are the best pets you can own.
   b. Cats are clean.
   c. Cats are independent.

   _____

   _____

3. **a.** Riding the bus is good for the environment.
   b. It is not convenient for everyone.
   c. This is because it is hard for disabled people to go up the stairs.
   d. This is because it is hard for disabled people to go down the stairs
   e. This is because it is hard for elderly people to go up the stairs.
   f. This is because it is hard for elderly people to go down the stairs.

   _____

   _____

Read the paragraph. Then follow the directions in the 10 steps to edit the information and composition of this paragraph. Write your revised paragraph on a separate sheet of paper. Be careful with capitalization and punctuation. Check your answers with the class.

DEFINITION PARAGRAPH

Plagiarism

[1] Dictionaries tell us that *plagiarism* is the act of using the words or ideas of another person as one's own or without identifying the original writer. [2] Plagiarism is serious. [3] In some cases, students are not permitted to continue at the school. [4] Students do not understand plagiarism. [5] However, according to Turnitin, which is a company that makes software that can find plagiarism, there are several types of plagiarism. [6] Two of these are very common among students. [7] With the first type, a student uses someone else's work. [8] An example of this is when a student pays someone to write a paper for a class. [9] The second most common type consists of a work that is not 100 percent original. [10] Both types of plagiarism are wrong. [11] The consequences are serious.

1. When making a list, it is common to use three items. In sentence 1, delete *or*. Then add *or other work* after the word *ideas* so the sentence has three items instead of just two. Add commas to the list of three items.

2. In sentence 2, add the word *very*.

3. In sentence 2, add the word *problem* and insert the article *a* in the correct place.

4. In sentence 2, it is not clear where the problem is. Add the phrase *at colleges and universities* after the word *problem*.

5. In sentence 4, since the statement is not true for all students, add *sometimes* to the beginning of the sentence.

6. In sentence 5, replace the word *several* with 10.

7. Replace the word *very* with *especially* in sentence 6.

8. In sentence 6, give more information about the students by adding the word *college*.

9. In sentence 8, change the word *paper* to *essay*. Change the article.

10. Combine sentences 10 and 11 using *so*.

Original Writing

On a separate sheet of paper, write a definition paragraph (at least five sentences) about a topic that interests you. Possible topics include:

- an ability that interests you, such as bilingualism
- a quality that you think is important for people to have, such as kindness
- a job that interests you
- something in nature that interests you, such as earthquakes or pandas

Explain what your topic is and give facts, details, and examples. Use at least one example of the verb *be* and underline it; try to use two if possible.

Here are some examples of how to begin.

- *Dictionaries tell us that bilingualism is the ability to use two languages, especially with equal or nearly equal fluency.*
- *El Niño is a complex weather pattern that occurs every two to seven years.*
- *A talent agent is a very important person in the movie industry.*

The Tokyo Metropolitan Government Building is the government headquarters for cities and towns in the Tokyo prefecture.

2 Using *Have* in Sentences

WHAT DO YOU KNOW?

DISCUSS Look at the photo and read the caption. Discuss the questions.

1. What famous government buildings does your capital city have?
2. Describe a building in your town or city that you like.

FIND THE ERRORS This paragraph contains two errors with the verb *have*. Find the errors and correct them. Explain your corrections to a partner.

The Japanese and American Systems of Government

[1] There have interesting similarities between the Japanese and American systems of government. [2] Like the United States, Japan has three independent branches: the legislative branch, the judicial branch, and the executive branch. [3] Both in Japan and in the United States, the legislative branch has the power to make laws. [4] In some ways, the legislative branch in Japan is similar to the U.S. legislative branch. [5] For example, the Japanese legislative branch has two houses: the House of Representatives and the House of Councillors. [6] The United States also have two houses: the Senate and the House of Representatives. [7] In short, the Japanese and American government systems are similar in several important areas.

Grammar Forms

2.1 Simple Present: *Have*

Subject	Verb	Example
I / you / we / they	*have*	Both Oman and United Arab Emirates **have** coastlines.
he / she / it /	*has*	Identity theft often **has** serious consequences for the victim.

2.2 Simple Past: *Have*

Subject	Verb	Example
I / he / she / it you / we / they	*had*	Afghanistan **had** two capitals until 1818. In the last century, Bolivia and Paraguay **had** a war over the Chaco region.

Notes
1. To form the negative, use *do/does/did + not + have*.
   A honeybee **does not have** a long life.
   At least nine U.S. presidents **did not have** a university education.
2. Contractions are almost never used in academic writing.

ACTIVITY 1

Fill in the blank with the correct form of *have*. Use *not* when it is there.

1. The president _____ the power to either sign a bill or to veto it.

2. Until 1928, only women over the age of 30 _____ the right to vote in England.

3. We only _____ accurate global temperature records after the year 1873.

4. Like England, India _____ a parliamentary form of government.

5. Before 1542, Japan _____ (*not*) much contact with the West.

6. Unlike the other planets, Mercury and Venus _____ (*not*) moons.

7. One of the goals of the United Nations is to increase the number of countries that _____ access to clean water.

8. Both of the latest development proposals _____ serious problems.

Common Uses

2.3	**Using *Have***

The verb *have* is commonly used in writing. It is used:

1. to show possession in the present or the past	McDonald's **has** about 35,000 locations worldwide.
	According to Professor Erik Asphaug, the earth **had** two moons several billion years ago.
	Most of the workers **did not have** proper safety equipment.
2. to show relationships among people	William Shakespeare **had** seven brothers and sisters.
	Photographer Ansel Adams **did not have** any siblings.
3. to show contents or qualities	Canada **has** more than 2 million lakes.
	The main character **did not have** much confidence.

ACTIVITY 2

Fill in the blank with the correct form of *have*. Use *not* when it is there.

1. The earth currently _____ a population of over 7 billion people.

2. There are two reasons why characters in Disney movies usually _____ (*not*) mothers.

3. A Chief Financial Officer _____ the responsibility of making financial plans and decisions for a company.

4. Countries near the equator, such as Singapore and Indonesia, _____ warm weather year-round.

5. Writing experts agree that a good story _____ five main elements: theme, plot, characters, conflict, and setting.

6. City College _____ more than 50 academic departments on 11 campuses.

7. After 1960, France _____ (*not*) control over Burkina Faso.

8. Before the nineteenth century, only a few American women _____ college degrees.

Common Errors

Common Error 2.1 Does the verb agree with the subject?

has
The United States ~~have~~ three branches of government.

have
Countries near the equator ~~has~~ two seasons—wet and dry.

has
The coastal area in both Oregon and California ~~have~~ a wide variety of plants and animals.

REMEMBER:
- Use *has* with *he*, *she*, *it*, and singular subjects in the present.
- Use *have* with *I*, *you*, and plural subjects in the present.
- Look for the main noun when a phrase comes between the subject and the verb.

ACTIVITY 3 **Common Error 2.1**

Underline the correct form of the verb.

1. Elephants in Africa (*has* / *have*) larger ears than Asian elephants.

2. Some experts claim that a child without any brothers or sisters sometimes (*has* / *have*) trouble making friends.

3. Unlike the rest of the country, cities on the southern coast of China (*has* / *have*) a mild climate.

4. Many people strongly believe that shopping online instead of in stores (*has* / *have*) important advantages.

5. City planners know that a city with a lot of parks usually (*has* / *have*) healthier residents.

6. Some companies, such as Google, (*has* / *have*) a good reputation because they treat their employees well.

7. According to the U.S. government, a citizen of two countries (*has* / *have*) the responsibility of following the laws of both countries.

8. Cities in Asia (*has* / *have*) more skyscrapers than in other parts of the world.

ACTIVITY 4 **Common Error 2.1**

In each paragraph, fill in the blank with the correct form of *have*. Use *not* when it is there.

1. The term *millennials* refers to the people born between 1980 and 2000. Fewer millennials, which is an important market group, currently _____ cars than did members of previous generations at the same age. This lower number is partly because many millennials _____ lower incomes compared with older generations at the same age. However, car-buying is increasing among millennials. Current research shows that social media _____ (*not*) very much influence on how millennials choose new cars.

2. According to the World Happiness Report of 2015, certain conditions lead to happiness. Countries that _____ these conditions are often at the top of world happiness lists. A typical Swiss resident, for example, _____ strong feelings of safety. A Swiss resident also usually _____ a deep sense of community. In fact, 86 percent of all Swiss feel that they _____ someone they can depend on if they need help.

3. Apes and humans _____ the same internal organs and the same types of bones. They also tend to suffer from the same types of diseases. Human and ape hands are similar, too. For example, the ape hand _____ an opposable thumb, which allows it to grip things. However, there are some physical differences between apes and humans. For example, apes _____ smaller brains than humans.

4. According to a Pew Research Center study on cell phones in Africa, South Africa _____ the greatest number of cell phone users. Approximately 90 percent of South Africans _____ a cell phone, and 34 percent of these South Africans _____ a smartphone. In contrast, Uganda _____ the fewest cell phones. In that country, 65 percent of the people _____ cell phones, and only 5 percent of these people _____ a smartphone.

Common Error 2.2   Do you need *have* or *be*?

is
Miami ~~has~~ the Florida city with the most people.

are
Most young children ~~have~~ afraid of the dark.

are
There ~~have~~ two official languages in the Philippines.

had
France ~~was~~ two capital cities during World War II.

REMEMBER:
- Use *be* to define a subject.
- Use *be* with words such as *born*, *years old*, *hungry*, *thirsty*, *tired*, *afraid*, *right*, and *lucky*.
- Use *be* with *there*.
- Use *have* to indicate possession or relationships.

ACTIVITY 5   **Common Error 2.2**

Underline the correct verb.

1. Xiamen, China, (*is* / *has*) a population of over 4 million people.

2. The Philippines (*is* / *has*) more than 7,000 islands.

3. According to some experts, parents should feed children only when they (*are* / *have*) hungry.

4. Starbucks (*was* / *had*) right to close shops that were not making enough money.

5. In 2015, Zimbabwe and Liberia (*were* / *had*) a very high unemployment rate.

6. There (*are* / *have*) three types of influenza: A, B, and C.

7. In 1930, there (*were* / *had*) 10 passenger ferries on San Francisco Bay.

8. Until 2016, only a few very special groups of Americans (*were* / *had*) the opportunity to travel to Cuba.

Academic Vocabulary

Nouns Frequently Used with *Have* in Academic Writing

access	consequences	difficulty	meaning	right
benefits	control	effect	opportunity	time

Source: Corpus of Contemporary American English (Davies 2008–)

ACTIVITY 6 **Vocabulary in Academic Writing**

Use the correct form of *have* and underline the correct academic vocabulary to complete the sentences. Include *not* when it is there.

Subject Area	Example from Academic Writing
Education	**1.** Teachers often _____ (*opportunity / difficulty*) controlling their classes unless they have strict rules.
Animal Behavior	**2.** The flu virus _____ serious (*consequences / benefits*) for wild pandas because it can kill them.
Business	**3.** According to many experts, you should not changes jobs unless you _____ (*an opportunity / a meaning*) for more responsibility and a higher salary.
Literature	**4.** Each word in a poem _____ (*meaning / access*). To understand the message of a poem, think about every possible meaning of each word.
Political Science	**5.** U.K. citizens _____ the (*effect / right*) to free speech. However, speech that insults people is illegal.
Health	**6.** According to the World Health Organization, 783 million people worldwide _____ (*not*) (*benefits / access*) to clean water.
English Composition	**7.** School uniforms _____ many (*rights / benefits*), including saving time and saving money.
Economics	**8.** For example, tourism _____ a positive (*effect / meaning*) on the economy of poor nations.
Nursing	**9.** Women over the age of 50 still _____ (*right / time*) to improve their bone health.
Psychology	**10.** When patients are experiencing stress, it is important to point out the things in their lives that they _____ (*access / control*) over, such as the food they eat or the people they spend time with.

Put It Together

Multiple Choice   Choose the letter of the correct answer.

1. There _____ at least three reasons why a college degree is important today.

   a. have   **b.** has   **c.** is   **d.** are

2. Unlike the university library, the public library _____ material for the general public.

   a. have   **b.** has   **c.** is   **d.** are

3. Both the China Institute and the Brooklyn Museum _____ Asian art.

   a. have   **b.** has   **c.** is   **d.** are

4. The walkway over the freeway is dangerous at night because it _____ enough lights.

   a. does not have   **b.** do not have   **c.** is not   **d.** are not

5. Beginning in 1921, American women _____ the right to vote.

   a. was   **b.** were   **c.** had   **d.** have

Error Correction   One of the five underlined words or phrases is not correct. Find the error and correct it. Be prepared to explain your answer.

6. Countries in tropical areas have hot and rainy almost every day, while countries in

   dry climates do not receive much rainfall.

7. The book version of *To Kill a Mockingbird* is similar to the movie version in that both

   has the same main characters and the same plot.

8. Benjamin Franklin had 22 years old and was the owner of his own printing business

   when he had his first child, William.

A coyote crosses a snowy field in a state park near Denver, Colorado.

Building Greater Sentences

Combine these short sentences into one sentence. You can add new words and move words around, but you should not add or omit any ideas. More than one answer is possible, but these sentences require the verb *have*. (See Appendix 1, Building Greater Sentences, page 206, for tips on how to do this activity.)

1. a. Wolves have physical features.
  b. Coyotes have physical features.
  c. These physical features are different.
  d. However, they have similar hunting styles.
  e. They also both have the ability to solve problems.

_____

_____

2. a. Meso-American pyramids are different from Egyptian pyramids.
  b. Meso-American pyramids have a flat top.
  c. Meso-American pyramids have steps up the sides.

_____

_____

3. a. Studying at a community college is a good idea.
  b. They have a variety of courses.
  c. It is a way to save money.
  d. You can save money before you attend a four-year college.

_____

_____

Steps to Composing

Read the paragraph. Then follow the directions in the 10 steps to edit the information and composition of this paragraph. Write your revised paragraph on a separate sheet of paper. Be careful with capitalization and punctuation. Check your answers with the class.

COMPARISON PARAGRAPH

Bees and Wasps

[1]To the average person, bees and wasps appear to be similar. [2]They are different in some interesting ways. [3]They have different diets, and they have different ways of defending themselves. [4]Bees and wasps also have some different physical features. [5]Bees have hair on their bodies and legs, while wasps do not. [6]Bees have flat, wide legs, while wasps have thinner, rounded legs. [7]Bees make honey. [8]Wasps are predators. [9]Bees are generally less aggressive than wasps. [10]Honeybees can sting one time, and then they die. [11]Other types of bees can sting more than once. [12]However, wasps are very aggressive, and they can sting several times.

---

1. Combine sentences 1 and 2 with the connector *but*.

2. In sentence 3, the subject and the verb (*they have*) are repeated. Change the sentence so that it will have only one subject and one verb. (Hint: Will you need the comma?)

3. In sentence 4, the word *some* is vague. Replace it with *several*.

4. In sentence 5, use the phrase *for example* or *for instance* to introduce the example.

5. In sentence 6, add the phrase *in addition* to introduce an additional example.

6. In sentence 7, explain what honey is. Add a comma after the word *honey* and this information: *which is their food*.

7. Sentence 8 has information that is very different from all the other information so far. Start with *in contrast* to show this difference.

8. Explain the word *predator* in sentence 8. After the word *predator*, put a comma and then add this information to give an example of how wasps are predators: *which means they catch and eat other insects*.

9. Sentence 9 is the last point of comparison in the paragraph. Begin the sentence with the word *finally* to connect this new information to the rest of the paragraph.

10. This paragraph does not have a concluding sentence. Add one sentence that restates the idea in the topic sentence in a different way.

ACTIVITY 10   Original Writing

On a separate sheet of paper, write a comparison paragraph (at least five sentences). Explain what the two things are and give facts, details, and examples. Use at least two examples of *have* or *has*. Underline your examples.

Here are some examples of how to begin.

- *Although a movie producer and a movie director are both important, a movie director is the more important role.*
- *Compared with other museums in San Francisco, the de Young Museum is one of the best places in the city to enjoy art, architecture, and treasures from around the world.*
- *There are many attractive college campuses in the world, but the University of Western Washington campus is one of the most beautiful campuses in the United States.*

A Chinese family enjoys *lao yu sheng* during a dinner to celebrate the Chinese Lunar New Year. Each person stands up and raises food with chopsticks for good luck.

3 Writing with the Simple Present

WHAT DO YOU KNOW?

DISCUSS Look at the photo and read the caption. Discuss the questions.

1. How do the people in the photo feel? Why?

2. How do celebrations add to our happiness?

FIND THE ERRORS This paragraph contains two errors with the simple present, including with *be*. Find the errors and correct them. Explain your corrections to a partner.

CAUSE-EFFECT PARAGRAPH

The Keys to Happiness

¹Why do some people always seem to be happy? ²Research show that happy people have certain habits. ³First of all, happy people smile a lot. ⁴They smile even if they are not happy. ⁵Smiling changes a person's attitude, experts say. ⁶Secondly, happy people eat well. ⁷They eat nutritious, high-energy foods and usually avoid processed and fast food. ⁸Happy people also live in the present. ⁹They do not reflect on the past or worry about the future. ¹⁰Furthermore, even though happy people tend to live in the present, they are very good at setting goals for themselves. ¹¹According to experts, having specific plans for things to look forward to also contribute to happiness.

Grammar Forms

3.1 Simple Present: *Be*

Subject	Verb	Example
I	*am*	I **am** a student at City College.
he / she / it	*is*	The official language of Brazil **is** Portuguese.
you / we / they	*are*	Both the Sumatran tiger and Siberian tiger **are** endangered species.

3.2 Simple Present: *There + Be*

In *There + be* sentences, the subject comes after the verb. *Be* agrees with the subject.

There + be	Example
There is + singular subject	**There is** new <u>information</u> about the train crash.
There are + plural subject	**There are** several <u>questions</u> about the experiment.

3.3 Simple Present: Verbs Other Than *Be*

Subject	Verb	Example
I / you / we / they	verb	The King and Queen of Sweden **live** in a palace just outside of Stockholm.
he / she / it	verb + *s*	The emperor penguin **lives** in the Antarctic.

3.4 Negative Present Forms

Form	Example
am / is / are + not	**I am not** a native speaker of English. There **is not** one easy way to learn a language. Rugby and cricket **are not** popular sports in the United States.
do / does not + verb	Elephants **do not have** good eyesight. The community college **does not require** SAT test scores.

Notes
1. Contractions are informal and are almost never used in academic writing.
2. Adverbs of frequency often appear with verbs in the present. They appear in specific positions in a sentence.

ACTIVITY 1

Fill in the blank with the correct form of the verb in parentheses. Use *not* when it is there.

1. Bilingualism _____ (*be*) the ability to speak two languages.

2. Wastewater and garbage _____ (*be*) two causes of ocean pollution.

3. The planet Mars _____ (*have*) two moons.

4. Political maps _____ (*show*) the borders between countries and states.

5. The playwright Tom Stoppard _____ (*not, be*) a native speaker of English.

6. A college degree _____ (*not, guarantee*) that you will get a good job.

7. Goosebumps _____ (*appear, sometimes*) on the skin when a person is cold or frightened.

8. Because the two insects look similar, it _____ (*be, often*) difficult to tell the difference between a centipede and a millipede.

Common Uses

The simple present is commonly used in academic writing:

1. to state facts or general truths that are not limited to a specific time	It **takes** eight minutes for light from the sun to reach the earth.
2. to describe habits and actions that occur regularly	The New York City subway system **runs** 24 hours a day.
3. to explain information from a story, a book, or a poem	In chapter 9 of *To Kill a Mockingbird*, Atticus **explains** why he decides to defend Tom.
4. with adverbs of frequency to describe how regularly habits or actions occur	Trains on the New York City subway system **are** usually crowded. Passengers often **complain** about delays on the subway.

Note

Use simple past for an event that happened and ended in the past.

The American Civil War **began** in 1861.

ACTIVITY 2

Underline the correct form of the verb.

1. Spanish (*is* / *was*) the official language of Mexico.

2. A day on Mars (*consists* / *consisted*) of 24 hours and 39 minutes.

3. During the Middle Ages, Muslims (*control* / *controlled*) Catalonia.

4. South Korean presidential elections (*occur* / *occurred*) every 5 years.

5. Afonso Pena (*becomes* / *became*) president of Brazil in 1908.

6. The Peak Tram in Hong Kong (*carries* / *carried*) over 11,000 people every day.

7. At the beginning of the first book, Harry Potter (*lives* / *lived*) in a cupboard under a staircase in the Dursely family home.

8. Suzanne Collins (*starts* / *started*) writing the The Hunger Games series in 2008.

Common Errors

Common Error 3.1 Do the subject and the verb agree?

prefer
Most South Korean sports fans ~~prefers~~ football over baseball.
  S   V

are
There ~~is~~ 36 states in Brazil.
  V   S

REMEMBER: • If the subject is singular, add -s, -es, or -ies to the base verb for the simple present. To help you choose the correct verb form (singular or plural), look for the main noun in the subject.

• With *there*, the subject comes after the verb.

ACTIVITY 3 Common Error 3.1

In each paragraph, fill in the blank with the correct form of the verb in parentheses.

1. The state of Maryland _____ (*have*) a mild climate. There _____ (*be*) about 213 days of sunny weather each year. It _____ (*rain*) approximately 42 days per year in the state. Snow _____ (*fall*) less often. For example, there _____ (*be*) 21.3 days of snowfall each year in Maryland. January _____ (*have*) the coldest weather, when the temperature _____ (*drop*) to the low 20s. The warmest weather in the state _____ (*occur*) in July, when temperatures _____ (*rise*) to the high 80s.

2. The book *Twilight*, by Stephenie Meyer, _____ (*be*) a love story between a teenaged girl and a vampire. When the story _____ (*begin*), the main character, Bella, _____ (*meet*) Edward. Edward _____ (*be*) a handsome, mysterious boy, and Bella _____ (*learn*) that he and his family _____ (*be*) vampires. Soon, Bella _____ (*fall*) in love with Edward. Then an evil vampire _____ (*come*) to town and _____ (*attack*) Bella, but Edward _____ (*save*) her.

Common Error 3.2   Is the verb *be* missing?

> is
> An exoskeleton ‸ a hard covering on the outside of an animal.
>
> *are*
> There ‸ two official languages in Canada.

REMEMBER: Use *be* to link ideas. All sentences must have a verb.

ACTIVITY 4   **Common Error 3.2**

Read each sentence. If the sentence is correct, write *C* on the line in front of the sentence. If *be* is missing, write *X* on the line. Then correct the sentence.

_____ **1.** There over 7 billion people on Earth today.

_____ **2.** There 1.01 men for every woman on Earth.

_____ **3.** Pluto 7.5 billion kilometers from Earth.

_____ **4.** The most common language in the world Mandarin.

_____ **5.** The quahog clam is the world's longest-living animal.

_____ **6.** News programs are the most popular types of shows in Brazil.

_____ **7.** Most users of social media in the United States female.

_____ **8.** A conservationist someone who works to protect the environment.

Common Error 3.3   Is the adverb in the correct position?

> *usually*
> Monarch butterflies spend ~~usually~~ ‸ the winter in Mexico.
>
> *never*
> Evergreen trees lose ‸ their leaves ~~never~~.
>
> *usually*
> November ~~usually~~ ‸ is the wettest month in Singapore.

REMEMBER: • Words like *usually, often, sometimes,* and *rarely* can appear at the beginning of the sentence or before the verb.

   • *Always* does not appear at the beginning or end of a sentence.

   • With *be*, adverbs of frequency usually appear after the verb.

Use the words given to write sentences. Put the adverbs in the correct position. More than one answer is possible.

1. often / to communicate with humans / use body language / cats / .

_____

2. to get a high-level job / sometimes / to have an MBA / it / necessary / is / .

_____

3. for services / in Japan / rarely / tip / people / .

_____

4. the largest female in the group / usually / the leader of an elephant herd / is / .

_____

5. above the Arctic Circle / never / the sun / sets / .

_____

6. recyclable / usually / are / glass containers / .

_____

7. a high school diploma / require / food service careers / usually / .

_____

8. International Women's Day / on March 8 / occurs / always / .

_____

Academic Vocabulary

Adverbs + Verbs Frequently Used in the Present in Academic Writing

always seem	never get	often find	sometimes feel	usually mean
always take	never know	often use	sometimes make	usually occur

Source: Corpus of Contemporary American English (Davies 2008–)

ACTIVITY 6 **Vocabulary in Academic Writing**

Use the correct present form of the verb in the academic vocabulary to complete the sentences. More than one answer may be possible.

Subject Area	Example from Academic Writing
Business	1. Sometimes an employee _____ mistakes if his or her manager does not clearly explain the goals of a project.
Opinion Essay	2. If you use social media, you should be careful in your postings because you never _____ who will see them.
Psychology	3. Shy, quiet people often _____ it difficult to participate in group activities.
Economics	4. Cheap oil usually _____ consumers have more money to spend.
Education	5. Communications teachers often _____ video to show good and bad use of body language in presentations.
Health	6. Sports injuries usually _____ when players do not warm up properly.
Media Studies	7. In many horror films, the villain never _____ caught, and viewers know he or she will return later to cause more problems.
Nursing	8. A patient who always _____ to be hungry may in fact not be getting enough sleep.
Sociology	9. Sometimes, young people _____ overwhelmed by stress and anxiety when they first leave home and go to college.
English Composition	10. For example, it always _____ a lot longer to graduate from college than most students expect.

Put It Together

Review Quiz

Multiple Choice   Choose the letter of the correct answer.

1. The temperature rarely _____ in climates that are near the equator.

   a. change   **b.** changes   **c.** changing   **d.** to change

2. Harper Lee _____ *To Kill a Mockingbird* over 50 years ago.

   a. is writing   **b.** writes   **c.** write   **d.** wrote

3. Garcia and Rodriguez _____ the most common last names in Mexico.

   a. are   **b.** be   **c.** has   **d.** is

4. _____ a good idea for drivers to turn off their cell phones when they get into the car.

   a. Always it is   **b.** Always there are **c.** It is always   **d.** There is always

5. Most people in Argentina _____ Spanish.

   a. to speak   **b.** speak   **c.** speaking   **d.** speaks

Error Correction   One of the five underlined words or phrases is not correct. Find the error and correct it. Be prepared to explain your answer.

6. One problem <u>many</u> older <u>people</u> <u>has</u> is the lack <u>of</u> convenient public transportation.

7. In the book version of *Twilight*, the <u>characters</u> Victoria, James, and Laurent <u>did not appear</u> until the

   end, <u>but</u> in the movie version, they <u>appear</u> <u>earlier</u> in the story.

8. <u>Never</u> it is <u>a good</u> idea <u>to study</u> for a test <u>at</u> the last minute, and recent studies <u>prove</u> this.

Schoolboys wear sun hats at a public school in New South Wales, Australia.

ACTIVITY 8 **Building Greater Sentences**

Combine these short sentences into one sentence. You can add new words and move words around, but you should not add or omit any ideas. More than one answer is possible, but these sentences require simple present verbs. (See Appendix 1, Building Greater Sentences, page 206, for tips on how to do this activity.)

1. **a.** Children in Australia often wear hats to school.
   b. Children do this when ultraviolet levels are high.
   c. Children do not need the hats in the winter months.
   d. The ultraviolet levels are usually low in these months.

2. **a.** Roses grow well in Portland, Oregon.   **c.** This is also because the winters are usually mild.
   b. This is because it rains a lot in the area. **d.** Another reason is the summers are warm.

3. **a.** At the beginning of the story, Harry Potter lives with his uncle's family.
   b. He is unhappy living with them.
   c. One day, he receives a letter that invites him to Hogwarts.

ACTIVITY 9 **Steps to Composing**

Read the paragraph. Then follow the directions in the 10 steps to edit the information and composition of the paragraph. Write your revised paragraph on a separate sheet of paper. Be careful with capitalization and punctuation. Check your answers with the class.

Digital Books vs. Printed Books

[1] Digital books are better than print books for college students. [2] Digital books are less expensive than printed textbooks. [3] For example, the price of a typical electronic version of a college psychology textbook is less than the print version. [4] Digital books are much more convenient than print books. [5] For example, the average textbook weighs almost four pounds. [6] An e-reader with several textbooks on it weighs less. [7] More learning takes place with digital books than with print textbooks. [8] This is because digital books can connect to dictionaries and the Internet, so students can look up words they do not know. [9] They can also get more background information on the topic they are reading about. [10] It is clear from these facts that digital books are superior to print books.

1. In sentence 1, add the phrase *in my opinion* to show it is the writer's opinion.

2. In sentence 2, add a word that shows this is the first reason.

3. In sentence 3, be more precise about the difference in price by adding *about 50 percent* (less).

4. In sentence 4, add a word to show that this is the second reason.

5. In sentence 6, add a detail that gives more information about the weight. (Hint: An e-reader weighs less than a half a pound, no matter how many books it contains.)

6. Combine sentences 5 and 6 to show a contrast. (Hint: Add *although*.)

7. In sentence 7, add a word that shows that this is the last idea in the list.

8. In sentence 8, change *words they do not know* to *unknown words*.

9. Combine sentences 8 and 9.

10. Make sentence 10 a little more precise by adding the phrase *for college students*.

ACTIVITY 10   Original Writing

On a separate sheet of paper, write an opinion paragraph (at least five sentences) about a topic that interests you. Support your opinion with facts and details. Use at least three examples of present verbs and underline them.

Here are some examples of how to begin.

- *In my opinion, shopping online is better than shopping in stores.*
- *There are three reasons why school uniforms are a good idea.*
- *The rule to ban sugary drinks in the campus café is a good idea for several reasons.*

A bicyclist rides in a special bike lane along the busy
Avenida Bernardino de Campos in São Paulo, Brazil.

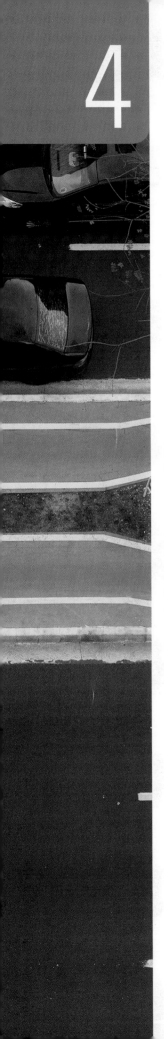

4 Writing with the Present Progressive

WHAT DO YOU KNOW?

DISCUSS Look at the photo and read the caption. Discuss the questions.

1. Does your city have bike lanes? Why or why not?
2. In what ways are bicycles a good idea in a city?

FIND THE ERRORS This paragraph contains two errors with the present progressive. Find the errors and correct them. Explain your corrections to a partner.

DESCRIPTIVE PARAGRAPH

Bike-Friendly Cities

[1] Today cities are making life easier for bike riders in a number of ways. [2] In many cases, cities are adding separate bike lanes along the main streets, and they increase the number of bike racks in public spaces, such as city centers and parks. [3] Large cities with bus transportation are installing bike carriers on the front of buses, and they are distributing maps that show where bike routes intersect with bus routes. [4] Some creative cities are building bike paths through green areas that are completely separate from automobile traffic. [5] These green areas are having benches and water fountains where a bike rider can stop to rest. [6] Since more and more people are riding bicycles today, city planners will need to look for additional ways to make their cities bike friendly.

Grammar Forms

4.1 Present Progressive

Subject	Verb	Example
I	*am* + (*not*) verb + *-ing*	I **am attending** night classes currently.
he / she / it	*is* + (*not*) verb + *-ing*	The elementary school **is not offering** art classes this year.
we / you / they	*are* + (*not*) verb + *-ing*	Because of the increase in mobile devices, businesses these days **are finding** new ways to advertise.

Notes

1. To form the negative, use *am/is/are* + *not* + verb + *-ing*.
   She **is not working** in Sweden this year.
   If the activity has stopped completely, use *no longer*.
   She **is no longer** working in Sweden.

2. Contractions are informal and are not usually used in academic writing.

3. When two or more progressive verbs are in a series and the subject is the same, you do not need to repeat the auxiliary *am/is/are*.
   The deer **are eating and sleeping** in people's yards.
   (They are eating *and* they are sleeping.)

4.2 Spelling Progressive Forms

1. Most verbs: use the base form of the verb + *-ing*.	*walk → walking*
2. Verbs that end in *-e*: drop the *-e* and add *-ing*.	*write → writing*
3. Verbs that end in *-ie*: change *-ie* to *-y* and add *-ing*.	*die → dying*
4. a. Verbs that end in consonant + vowel + consonant: double the final consonant and add *-ing*. b. Do not double the final consonant when the last syllable is not stressed (for example, *O-pen* or *LI-sten*). c. Do not double *-w, -x,* or *-y*.	*run → running* *begin → beginning* *open → opening* *listen → listening* *showing, fixing, playing*

4.3 Position of Adverbs

Position	Example
1. Words like *today, now, nowadays, at this time, these days, this week,* and *this year* can be placed at the beginning or end of the sentence.	Wildlife biologists are tracking grizzly bears **this year**.
2. Other words like *currently* and *presently* can be placed at the beginning, middle, or end of the sentence. When the adverb is in the middle, it is placed between the two parts of the verb.	**Presently**, the approval rating of the president is going up. The highway department is **currently** building fences to protect deer.
3. *Still* and *no longer* are placed between the two parts of the verb.	For economic reasons, many people are **still** living without access to health care.

ACTIVITY 1

In each sentence, underline the present progressive verb and any time words. Label the subject of the verb with *S*. The first item is done for you.

1. Computer programmers <u>are creating</u> new security software <u>nowadays</u>.

2. These days, major U.S. banks are charging customers a fee for a savings account.

3. Even though the city created separate bike lanes, cyclists are still using the roads.

4. Recently, Americans are spending more and more money on pet supplies.

5. What is happening in our schools today?

6. Engineers are currently working on ways to prevent another nuclear accident.

7. People are concerned about what they eat, and today many consumers are demanding better information about the food they purchase.

8. Many people are buying and selling gold coins as an investment these days.

Common Uses

4.4 Using Present Progressive

The present progressive is commonly used:

1. to describe an activity in progress currently (over a period of time), but not necessarily at this exact moment
 	
  a. extended present
 	
  b. temporary (not permanent)
 	
• This is common in reports, news, letters, and e-mails.
• It is used with time words like *these days, this semester, currently.*

	PAST NOW FUTURE
	
	The president **is visiting** two foreign countries <u>this week</u>.
	
	I **am looking** forward to touring the university campus.

2. to indicate a present situation that is changing • This is common in describing trends and surveys. • It is used with quantity adverbs like *more and more, more than ever, fewer,* and *less.*	 PAST NOW FUTURE Since the cost of parking **is increasing**, <u>more and more</u> people **are sharing** rides to work and school. People **are drinking** <u>more</u> coffee <u>than ever</u> before.
3. to emphasize a repeated action • It is often used with *always, continually,* or *still.* • It can express irritation.	 PAST NOW FUTURE Politicians **are** <u>always</u> **promising** something. Most places have Internet security, but certain crafty hackers **are** <u>still</u> **getting** into computer systems.
4. to express an active meaning of a stative (nonactive) verb • Some verbs such as *have, smell, taste, feel, look, be,* and *think* have two meanings: one active and one stative.	*active* The company **is looking** for a new location. *stative* The sky **looks** smoky. *active* Due to the drought, some animals **are having** a hard time finding water. *stative* Cheetahs **have** spots on their fur.

Notes
1. In academic writing, the simple present is much more common than the progressive.
2. Health care workers commonly use present progressive to describe what is happening at the moment. The patient **is sleeping** comfortably.
3. Most stative (nonactive) verbs are not usually used in the progressive. Stative verbs express:
   a. possession (*own, belong, include, have*)
   b. description (*sound, smell, taste, feel, look, be*)
   c. emotion (*like, love, hate, want, need*)
   d. belief (*know, believe, seem, doubt, agree, disagree, think*)

ACTIVITY 2

Fill in the blank with the present progressive form of the verb in parentheses. Be careful of spelling.

1. Ecotourism is popular now, and more people _____ (*travel*) to destinations like the Galapagos than ever before.

2. Because photography is a popular hobby these days, more and more people _____ (*buy*) cameras.

3. At this time, scientists from around the world _____ (*talk about*) ways to live with climate change.

4. According to the most recent report, the Forest Service _____ (*send*) 300 firefighters to assist the current Montana team.

5. By studying the soil from Mars, scientists _____ (*try*) to discover whether life existed on the Red Planet.

6. More and more minority languages _____ (*die*) these days due to political, social, and economic reasons.

7. Basam has enrolled in the Sports Medicine program, and he _____ (*look*) forward to the start of classes.

8. It is sad that computer hackers _____ always _____ (*find*) new ways to break codes.

9. Wind farms _____ (*gain*) popularity with locals in South Africa as a way to create energy.

10. Campus administrators _____ (*take*) steps to install more bike racks.

Common Errors

Common Error 4.1 Is the present progressive form correct?

are drilling
Petroleum companies ~~drilling~~ for oil.

hiring
Petroleum companies are ~~hire~~ new employees.

are
Companies ~~is~~ expanding quickly.

REMEMBER: • Use *be* + verb + *-ing*.

• Check for subject–verb agreement.

ACTIVITY 3 **Common Error 4.1**

In each sentence, underline the verb. If the verb form is correct, write *C* on the line. If it is wrong, write *X* on the line. Then write the correction above the sentence.

_____ **1.** Right now, people and animals in Alaska experiencing their warmest winter since 1800.

_____ **2.** According to three recent reports, ocean temperatures are becoming warmer.

_____ **3.** Even though it is illegal, poachers in Africa is still killing elephants for their ivory tusks.

_____ **4.** Airplane manufacturers is no longer building supersonic airliners due to their high fuel use.

_____ **5.** The city of Venice, Italy, is slowly sinking into the bay.

_____ **6.** Biologists from Georgia Tech is learning how ants live through floods.

_____ **7.** Unfortunately, the Aral Sea in Central Asia is rapidly dry up.

_____ **8.** Currently, architects are working on new ways to make houses more energy efficient.

Common Error 4.2 Is the spelling correct?

writing
The team is ~~writeing~~ a new research proposal.

REMEMBER: Use the correct spelling for progressive forms. In this case, the verb ends in *-e*. Drop the *-e* and add *-ing*.

Common Error 4.2

Fill in the blank with the present progressive form of the verb in parentheses. Be careful with spelling.

1. Due to climate change, tornadoes _____ (*occur*) more frequently.

2. Biologists _____ (*continue*) to investigate the effects of warmer oceans.

3. Coral reefs _____ (*die*) because of coastal development.

4. More and more farmers _____ (*cut*) down trees in order to create larger areas for their crops.

5. Some experts wonder whether smart technology _____ (*make*) us less intelligent.

Common Error 4.3 **Do you need simple present or present progressive?**

> *beats*
> The human heart ~~is beating~~ 100,000 times per day.

REMEMBER: Use the simple present for habits, routines, or facts that occur every day, every year, or all the time.

ACTIVITY 5 **Common Error 4.3**

Fill in the blanks with the correct form of the verbs in parentheses.

1. Many women in traditional Senegal villages _____ (*stay*) near their homes. However, today many of them _____ (*start*) a new forest by planting trees miles away from home.

2. Generally, a person _____ (*buy*) a house in order to have a place to live. However, these days more and more people _____ (*buy*) houses as investments in the hope of making money.

3. Because of large wildlife reserves in China, the Giant Panda population _____ (*increase*). This _____ (*be*) a success story since Giant Pandas rarely _____ (*give*) birth in zoos.

4. Every spring at a church in San Juan Capistrano, California, thousands of birds _____ (*return*) to make their nests. This is a famous event that tourists _____ (*come*) to watch every year. This year, however, the birds _____ (*not, find*) enough food.

Common Error 4.4   Is it a stative verb?

> *includes*
> The National Geographic Big Cat Project ~~is including~~ lions, leopards, and cheetahs.

REMEMBER: Use the simple present with stative (nonactive) verbs that describe a present state or condition.

ACTIVITY 6   **Common Error 4.4**

Fill in the blank with the correct simple present or present progressive form of the verb in parentheses. Use *not* when it is there.

1. Film director James Cameron _____ (*love*) to dive in deep water, so he _____ (*create*) a new underwater film.

2. Currently, the city council members _____ (*agree*) that the future _____ (*look*) good for investors.

3. Nowadays people _____ (*want*) to eat healthy food, so many farmers _____ (*think about*) growing more organic crops.

4. Honey bees _____ (*disappear*), and some scientists _____ (*think*) they know the reasons.

5. Some people _____ (*not, believe*) that the earth's climate _____ (*change*).

6. Very few people _____ (*know*) that killer whales actually _____ (*belong*) to the dolphin family.

7. These days, many college students _____ (*need*) to find a part-time job since the cost of living _____ (*increase*).

8. Because of food allergies, many people these days _____ (*eat*) gluten-free bread, and they say it _____ (*taste*) just as good as bread with gluten.

Academic Vocabulary

Verbs Frequently Used in Present Progressive in Academic Writing

become	do	take	use
begin	make	try	work

Source: Corpus of Contemporary American English (Davies 2008–)

ACTIVITY 7   **Vocabulary in Academic Writing**

Use the academic vocabulary in the present progressive to complete the sentences. For some sentences, more than one answer is possible.

Subject Area	Example from Academic Writing
Finance	**1.** Many corporate executives have doubts about startup companies, but aggressive CEOs _____ greater risks with their companies these days.
Environmental Science	**2.** Maintaining clean water sources is important, so some concerned citizens from Rochester, New York, _____ together to clean trash out of streams that flow into the Erie Canal.
Health	**3.** According to a recent report, a new asthma medicine looks hopeful for the future because it _____ to improve the lives of older patients.
English Composition	**4.** A simile compares two dissimilar things. For example, when an author says a person is like a tree, he or she _____ a simile to make a vivid description.
English Literature	**5.** In *Hoot*, some teenagers _____ to stop people from building a restaurant where an owl's nest is located.
Education	**6.** It is important for teachers to see whether students _____ the assignments correctly so that they know whether to provide additional explanations.
English Composition	**7.** For several very important reasons, doctors believe that many offices _____ employees sick.
Computer Science	**8.** Because of satellites and new frequencies, global communication systems _____ faster and faster. However, consumers want more than speed. They also want lower prices and the ability to have multiple devices connected at the same time.

Put It Together

Multiple Choice   Choose the letter of the correct answer.

1. Canadian geese _____ south every fall.

   a. are flying   **b.** fly   **c.** flies   **d.** is flying

2. Dr. Murray Salby, a well-known climatologist, _____ a paper about the causes of global warming.

   a. are writing   **b.** write   **c.** writes   **d.** is writing

3. Governor Jerry Brown of California said, "I _____ that we need to conserve water!"

   a. am agree   **b.** agree   **c.** am agreeing   **d.** is agreeing

4. Llamas, an important South American animal, _____ to the same family as camels from Asia.

   a. are belonging   **b.** belongs   **c.** belong   **d.** is belonging

5. If the audio _____ on that webpage, you need to update your software.

   a. not is working   **b.** not working   **c.** not works   **d.** is not working

Error Correction   One of the five underlined words or phrases is not correct. Find the error and correct it. Be prepared to explain your answer.

6. According to the Association of Zoos, elephants only needing an area the size of nine parking spots, but conservationists agree that elephants require a larger area.

7. In Southeast Asia, yellow snails is destroying wetlands plants and causing millions of dollars in damage to rice crops. As a result, community members are working together to remove the snails by hand.

8. More and more people in China are eating in fast-food restaurants because of recent lifestyle changes. People in China now are having more money to spend, but unfortunately they are working longer and longer hours to get it.

The Jacob and Wilhelm Grimm Center at Humboldt University in Berlin, Germany, has 12 separate libraries.

Building Greater Sentences

Combine these short sentences into one sentence. You can add new words and move words around, but you should not add or omit any ideas. More than one answer is possible, but these sentences require present progressive.

1. a. Librarians use technology.
   b. Technology is used to manage data.
   c. There are large amounts of data.
   d. It is these days.

_____

_____

2. a. People are using their smart phones.
   b. They are using them as computers.
   c. They are using them as cameras.
   d. They are doing this more and more.

_____

_____

3. a. Home gardeners save seeds.
   b. The seeds are from their favorite tomato plants.
   c. This is happening nowadays.
   d. This is happening more and more.

_____

_____

Read the paragraph. Then follow the directions in the 10 steps to edit the information and composition of this paragraph. Write your revised paragraph on a separate sheet of paper. Be careful with capitalization and punctuation. Check your answers with the class.

CAUSE-EFFECT PARAGRAPH

Changes in the American Diet

[1]Americans are eating less meat. [2]The reason people are eating less meat is that they are worried about their health. [3]People want to be healthier. [4]People want to live longer. [5]Many people are concerned about high cholesterol, so they are eating meat substitutes like veggie burgers. [6]Also, people are worried that certain kinds of meat cause cancer. [7]Besides health concerns, Americans are buying less meat because the price of meat is rising. [8]Finally, concern for the environment is causing people to eat less meat. [9]It takes more energy to produce beef than grain. [10]Whether it is for health or money, Americans are eating less meat.

---

1. In sentence 1, not all Americans are eating less meat. Add the word *many* in the correct place.

2. In this short paragraph the verb *eat* occurs five times. It is not good to repeat one word so often. In sentence 2, change *eating less meat* to *making this change*.

3. The writer gives several reasons, not just one, why people are eating less meat. In sentence 2, change *The reason* to *The number one reason*.

4. *People* is the subject of both sentences 3 and 4. Use the subject pronoun in sentence 4.

5. Begin sentence 5 with the word *nowadays*.

6. In sentence 6, change the opening word *also* to the phrase *in addition*.

7. Sentence 6 needs an example of the type of meat, so add the phrase *such as sausage* after the word *meat*.

8. In sentence 6, the verb *cause* sounds very strong, so add the word *can* or *might* to soften the verb.

9. In the last sentence, the writer forgot to mention the third reason, so add the phrase *the environment* in the correct place. Use commas to list the reasons.

10. Not all Americans are eating less meat. In the last sentence, add the phrase *a large number of* in the correct place.

ACTIVITY 11 **Original Writing**

On a separate sheet of paper, write a descriptive paragraph (at least five sentences) about a current trend. Use at least one example of present progressive and underline it. Try to use two examples.

Here are some examples of how to begin.

- *Technology is changing our daily lives.*
- *The need for health care workers is growing.*
- *The rainforest in . . . is disappearing.*

This 13th-century illustration shows travelers on their way to Mecca.

وَكَادَ يَنْزِعُ لِلْجِمَالِ النَّمَرَ وَأَنْشَدَ

الْحَجِّ سَبِيلَكَ تَأَوِّيًا وَاِدْلَاجًا وَلَا تَعَيَّا لَكُمْ أَجْمَالًا وَاحِدَاجًا

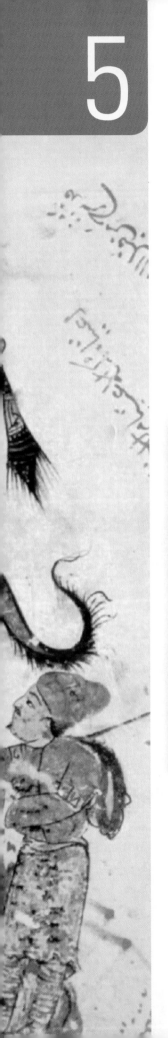

5 Writing with the Simple Past

WHAT DO YOU KNOW?

DISCUSS Look at the illustration and read the caption. Discuss the questions.

1. How did people travel in the thirteenth century? What did they bring?

2. What can we learn from the stories of travelers in ancient times?

FIND THE ERRORS This paragraph contains two errors with the simple past. Find the errors and correct them. Explain your corrections to a partner.

NARRATIVE PARAGRAPH (BIOGRAPHY)

Ibn Battuta, World Traveler

¹Ibn Battuta was one of the world's greatest travelers. ²He was born in Tangier, Morocco, in 1304, and he came from a family of Islamic scholars. ³One day in 1325, Battuta left home. ⁴He wanted to make a pilgrimage to Mecca. ⁵However, instead of going home after Mecca, he continued his journey, and he did not returned to Morocco for many years. ⁶Over his lifetime, Battuta traveled for 29 years and covers over 75,000 miles. ⁷He traveled throughout the Middle East, Africa, and Asia. ⁸Battuta had many exciting adventures on his travels. ⁹For example, he saw a rhinoceros and a hippopotamus for the first time. ¹⁰Thieves attacked him in India. ¹¹Battuta wrote about his journeys when he got home. ¹²Today we know a lot about life in the fourteenth century, thanks partly to Ibn Battuta.

Grammar Forms

5.1 Simple Past

Subject	Verb	Example
I / you / he / she / it / we / they	a. regular verb + -ed	European explorers to California **included** Hernán Cortes, Sir Francis Drake, and Sebastián Viscaíno.
	b. irregular verb	The Mexican–American War **began** in 1846.

Notes

1. For regular past verbs, add -ed. (work → work**ed**), -d (live → live**d**), or change the y to i and add -ed (deny → den**ied**). If the verb ends in a consonant + vowel + consonant, double the last consonant before adding -ed (stop → stop**ped**).
2. Here are some irregular verbs commonly used in academic writing, listed in order of frequency. See Appendix 4, Irregular Verbs, page 210, for a more complete list.

be → was, were	make → made	begin → began	take → took
have → had	say → said	come → came	find → found
do → did	become → became		

5.2 Simple Past: *Be*

Subject	Verb	Example
I / he / she / it	*was* (irregular)	George III **was** King of England for 59 years.
you / we / they	*were* (irregular)	Benjamin Franklin and Thomas Paine **were** important writers during the American Revolution.

5.3 Negative Past Forms

Form	Example
did not + verb	George Washington **did not live** in the White House. The study **did not find** that stress causes heart disease.
was / were + not	California **was not** a state until 1850. Burundi and Chad, two African countries, **were not** part of the British Empire.

Fill in the blank with the correct form of the verb in parentheses. Use *not* when it is there.

1. The photographer Ansel Adams _____ (*die*) on April 22, 1984.

2. Reality TV _____ (*not, become*) popular worldwide until the early 2000s.

3. Dutch traders first _____ (*come*) to Japan in the early seventeenth century.

4. In 1865, the Thirteenth Amendment _____ (*end*) slavery in the United States.

5. The Industrial Revolution _____ (*begin*) in the early nineteenth century.

6. According to Steve Wozniak, Steve Jobs _____ (*not, help*) design the first Apple computers.

7. Most public schools _____ (*not, have*) computers before the 1980s.

8. A powerful earthquake _____ (*occur*) in Nepal in 2015.

An ancient temple collapsed during a 7.8 earthquake in Nepal in April of 2015.

Common Uses

5.4 Using the Simple Past

The simple past is commonly used in writing. It is used:

1. to describe an action or a condition that was completed in the past	The French Revolution **started** in 1789.
2. to describe a series of completed actions.	Danish women **got** the vote in 1915, and American women **won** the vote in 1920.
3. to show causes and effects in the past	The cost of fruits and vegetables **rose** because there **was** a drought.

ACTIVITY 2

Fill in the blank with the correct form of the verb in parentheses. Use simple past or simple present.

1. The fashion designer Christian Dior _____ (*introduce*) the "New Look," dresses with longer hemlines, in 1947.

2. The dodo bird _____ (*become*) extinct in the seventeenth century.

3. Walt Disney _____ (*move*) to Hollywood in 1923, and he _____ (*start*) the Walt Disney Company in 1925.

4. Sir William Herschel _____ (*discover*) the planet Uranus in 1781, and John Couch Adams _____ (*identify*) Neptune in 1846.

5. Tornadoes frequently _____ (*occur*) in the central part of the United States.

6. According to some experts, dinosaurs _____ (*disappear*) because global temperatures _____ (*drop*).

7. During her father's lifetime, Elizabeth II often _____ (*represent*) George VI in public events because he _____ (*be*) ill.

8. Print textbooks _____ (*be*) often more expensive than digital textbooks.

Common Errors

Common Error 5.1   Do you need simple present or simple past?

won
The Brazilians ~~win~~ the World Cup in 2014.

occur
The World Cup games ~~occurred~~ every four years.

have
The World Cup games usually ~~had~~ more viewers than the Olympics.

REMEMBER: • Use the simple past to describe an action or a condition that was completed in the past.

• Use the simple present to describe facts or general truths, habits, and to explain information from a story, a book, or a poem.

ACTIVITY 3   Common Error 5.1

Fill in the blank with the correct simple past or simple present form of the verb in parentheses.

1. From 1271 to 1295, Marco Polo _____ (*travel*) from Europe to Asia.

2. To apply for a U.S. passport, you _____ (*need*) proof of citizenship, identity documents, and two passport photos.

3. On Mount Waialeale, which is in Hawaii, it _____ (*rain*) 129.73 inches in 2014.

4. In Mawsynram, Meghalaya, India, there _____ (*be*) about 467.4 inches of rain each year.

5. Until the nineteenth century, most Europeans _____ (*think*) tomatoes were poisonous.

6. At the beginning of the first Harry Potter book, Harry _____ (*be*) 10 years old.

7. J. K. Rowling, the author of the Harry Potter series, _____ (*grow up*) in Chepstow, Gwent, United Kingdom.

8. In 1849, John Muir _____ (*immigrate*) to the United States.

9. Muir _____ (*became*) a famous naturalist, author, and philosopher.

10. He hiked throughout the Yosemite area, and today many people _____ (*enjoy*) hiking on the same trails in Yosemite National Park.

Common Error 5.2   Do you use the correct form?

lived
Marco Polo ~~was live~~ in China for 17 years.

brought
In the Middle Ages, Muslims ~~bringed~~ sugar to Europe.

REMEMBER: To form the simple past, add *-ed* or use the correct irregular verb past form. Do not use *was* or *were* + verb.

ACTIVITY 4   **Common Error 5.2**

In each sentence, underline the past verb form. If the verb form is correct, write *C* on the line. If it is wrong, write *X* on the line. Then cross out the error and write the correct word above it.

_____ **1.** Henry Mill was invent the first typewriter in 1714.

_____ **2.** Thomas Sutherland started the Hong Kong and Shanghai Banking Corporation Limited (HSBC) in 1865.

_____ **3.** During the sixteenth century, most Europeans thinked potatoes were dangerous to eat.

_____ **4.** Europeans were come to Brazil at the beginning of the sixteenth century.

_____ **5.** The Zapotec people of Mexico built the city of Teotihuacán between 100 BC and AD 700.

_____ **6.** Greece and Italy were not part of the North Atlantic Treaty Organization (NATO) until 1952.

_____ **7.** During the Great Depression, some famous American authors were write books about American life for $20 a week.

_____ **8.** Valentina Tereshkova become the first woman to go into space in 1962, when she flew a Russian spacecraft around the earth 48 times.

Common Error 5.3   Are your verb tenses consistent?

was
People thought the luxury steamship *RMS Titanic* ~~is~~ safe because it was so big.

invented
Benjamin Franklin enjoyed swimming in cold water, and he ~~invents~~ the first swim fins when he was 11 years old.

REMEMBER: Use the simple past to describe an action or a condition that was completed in the past.

ACTIVITY 5 **Common Error 5.3**

In each paragraph, fill in the blank with the correct form of the verb in parentheses. Use *not* when it is there.

1. Rosalind Elsie Franklin _____ (*make*)
    important contributions to the field of molecular biology. She
    _____ (*be*) born in London, England, in 1920.
    She _____ (*attend*) an all-girls school in
    London, and she _____ (*do*) well in science
    classes. When she _____ (*be*) 15 years old,
    she _____ (*decide*) to become a scientist.
    Franklin _____ (*have*) to work very hard
    to convince her father to let her go to Cambridge University because he
    _____ (*not, believe*) in higher education for women,
    and he _____ (*not, want*) her to become a scientist.

2. During the years of segregation in the United States, it
    _____ (*be*) difficult for African-Americans to travel.
    Throughout the United States, and especially in the South, most hotels and
    restaurants _____ (*not, allow*) African-Americans to
    enter. Because many African-Americans _____ (*travel*)
    for business or pleasure, in 1936, Victor H. Green, a New York City mailman,
    _____ (*decide*) to publish a guide book to help them. *The
    Negro Motorist Green Book* _____ (*include*) information
    on hotels, restaurants, gas stations, and hair salons throughout the country that
    _____ (*be*) safe for African-Americans to visit. The
    last edition of *The Negro Motorist Green Book* _____
    (*appear*) in 1966, two years after Congress _____
    (*pass*) the Civil Rights Act.

Common Error 5.4   Is the negative form correct?

> *accept*
> Harvard did not ~~accepted~~ women until 1879.
>
> *wear*
> Public school students did not ~~wore~~ uniforms in the1950s.

REMEMBER: To form the simple past negative for both regular and irregular verbs, use *did* + *not* + base form of verb.

ACTIVITY 6   **Common Error 5.4**

Fill in the blank with the correct negative form of the verb in parentheses.

1. Before 1660, clocks _____ (*have*) a minute hand.

2. Women in Japan _____ (*vote*) until 1945.

3. Abraham Lincoln, the sixteenth president of the United States,

_____ (*attend*) college.

4. Most drivers _____ (*use*) seatbelts until the
late 1950s.

5. Before 1200, Western number systems _____
(*include*) zero.

6. Contrary to popular belief, Apple _____ (*make*) its
first computers in a garage.

7. Most historians agree that George Washington _____
(*wear*) dentures made from wood.

8. University of California students who were state residents

_____ (*have*) to pay tuition until 1970.

Academic Vocabulary

Verbs Frequently Used in Simple Past in Academic Writing

associate	be	have	make	report
base	do	include	provide	say

Source: Corpus of Contemporary American English (Davies 2008–)

ACTIVITY 7 **Vocabulary in Academic Writing**

Use the simple past form of the correct academic vocabulary in parentheses to complete the sentences. Use *not* when it is there.

Subject Area	Example from Academic Writing
Sociology	1. The majority of the students in the 2001 survey _____ (*have / be*) female.
Education	2. In the 1950s, elementary school children _____ (*not, make / not, do*) as much homework as they do today.
History	3. Past Canadian prime ministers who were bilingual _____ (*base / include*) Pierre Elliott Trudeau and Paul Martin.
Literature	4. Jon Krakauer _____ (*say / base*) his book *Into the Wild* on his own experiences in Alaska.
Business	5. In 1886, an Atlanta pharmacist _____ (*make / do*) a carbonated drink to serve at his pharmacy that later became Coca-Cola.
Health	6. In the Middle Ages, people _____ (*not, report / not, associate*) cleanliness with health.
Media Studies	7. The 2014 Status of Women in the U.S. Media _____ (*include / report*) that 90 percent of all sports publications have white males as editors.
Nursing	8. During the American Civil War, Catholic nuns _____ (*provide / associate*) nursing services in field hospitals.
Sociology	9. Until 1973, many American women _____ (*not, be / not, have*) the right to serve on a jury.
English Composition	10. As Nelson Mandela _____ (*say / base*) in 1990, "Education is the most powerful weapon which you can use to change the world."

Put It Together

Multiple Choice   Choose the letter of the correct answer.

1. Cai Lun, a Chinese official during the Han Dynasty, _____ paper in AD 105.

    a. invent   **b.** invented   **c.** invents   **d.** is inventing

2. J. K. Rowling _____ Harry Potter while she was teaching English in Portugal.

    a. is writing   **b.** writes   **c.** write   **d.** wrote

3. An adult giraffe _____ about 100 pounds of leaves each day.

    a. ate   **b.** eat   **c.** eats   **d.** was eating

4. Mark Zuckerberg started Facebook in 2004, and he _____ out of Harvard University the next year.

    a. dropping   **b.** drops   **c.** drop   **d.** dropped

5. The search engine BackRub _____ Google in 1998.

    a. became   **b.** becomes   **c.** become   **d.** was becoming

Error Correction   One of the five underlined words or phrases is not correct.
Find the error and correct it. Be prepared to explain your answer.

6. In the ancient Greek society of Sparta, male children slept outside and hunt for

    their own food.

7. People did not thought that the world was flat when Columbus sailed to the

    New World.

8. Many historians think that people played a early version of chess in India between

    AD 280 and 550.

A big asteroid crashes into the surface of an Earth-like planet in this artist's illustration.

ACTIVITY 9   **Building Greater Sentences**

Combine these short sentences into one sentence. You can add new words and move words around, but you should not add or omit any ideas. More than one answer is possible, but these sentences require simple past verbs.

1. a. A giant asteroid crashed into Earth.
   b. This happened about 65 million years ago.
   c. The crash changed the planet's temperature.

_____

_____

2. a. Chinese-American author Ha Jin immigrated to the United States.
   b. This happened in 1986.
   c. After that, he earned a PhD from Brandeis University.
   d. He also wrote several novels.

_____

_____

3. a. The bubonic plague killed over 25 million people.
   b. This was in the Middle Ages.
   c. The reason was that fleas caught the disease.
   d. Then the fleas gave the disease to humans.

_____

_____

Read the paragraph. Then follow the directions in the 10 steps below to edit the information and composition of this paragraph. Write your revised paragraph on a separate sheet of paper. Be careful with capitalization and punctuation. Check your answers with the class.

NARRATIVE PARAGRAPH (BIOGRAPHY)

Marie Curie

[1] In my opinion, one of the most important people in the history of science was Marie Curie. [2] Madame Curie made important discoveries at a time when it was difficult for women to succeed in science. [3] Marie Curie was born Maria Sklodowska in Poland in 1867. [4] Her father was a secondary school teacher. [5] He introduced his daughter to science. [6] When Madame Curie was 24 years old, she went to Paris to study at the Sorbonne. [7] At the Sorbonne, she received degrees in physics and math. [8] At the Sorbonne, she met her husband Pierre Curie and she married him. [9] Madame Curie did experiments with radioactivity. [10] Based on this work, she and her husband discovered two elements, radium and polonium, in 1898. [11] Both radium and polonium became important medical therapies. [12] In 1903, Curie became was the first woman to receive the Nobel Prize in physics. [13] She won a second Nobel Prize in 1911 for chemistry.

---

1. In sentence 2, use *significant* instead of *important* to avoid repetition.

2. Combine sentences 4 and 5 with *and*.

3. In sentence 5, replace *science* with *physics and chemistry* to be more specific.

4. Combine sentences 6 and 7 by replacing *At the Sorbonne* with *where*. (Hint: Put a comma after *Sorbonne* in sentence 6, before *where*.)

5. In sentence 8, delete *and she married him*. After *she met* insert *and married*.

6. In sentence 9, replace *did* with *conducted*.

7. Combine sentences 9 and 10 with *and*. (Hint: Use a comma between the two clauses.)

8. In sentence 11, replace *radium and polonium* with *these elements* to avoid repetition.

9. After sentence 11, add a sentence to give a specific example of how the elements became important medical therapies. (Hint: We use radium today in cancer therapy.)

10. Combine sentences 12 and 13 with *and*.

ACTIVITY 11 **Original Writing**

On a separate sheet of paper, write a narrative paragraph (at least five sentences) about a famous person or an important event that occurred in the past. Describe the person or event using facts, details, and examples. Use at least two examples of the simple past and underline them.

Here are some examples of how to begin.

- *Because she works hard for human rights, the person I admire most is Malala Yousafzai.*

- *Many people may not know this, but Leonardo da Vinci had a reading disability.*

- *One of the most important events in American history was the signing of the Civil Rights Act in 1964.*

U.S.-born photographer Mariana Yampolsky poses in her home in the Tlalpan neighborhood of Mexico City in 1993.

6 Writing with the Past Progressive

WHAT DO YOU KNOW?

DISCUSS Look at the photo and read the caption. Discuss the questions.

1. What was Yampolsky doing when the photographer took the photo?

2. What do you like to take photos of? Describe one of your best photos.

FIND THE ERRORS This paragraph contains two errors with the past progressive. Find the errors and correct them. Explain your corrections to a partner.

NARRATIVE PARAGRAPH BIOGRAPHY

Mariana Yampolsky

[1] Mariana Yampolsky was one of Mexico's greatest photographers. [2] She was born in Chicago, Illinois, in 1925. [3] Yampolsky studied at the University of Chicago, and she received a degree in social sciences. [4] However, she was always interested in Mexico and in Mexican art, so in 1945, after college, she moved to Mexico City. [5] She worked as a printmaker in Mexico City while she was learning to speak Spanish. [6] While she was make prints at Taller de Gráfica Popular (People's Graphics Workshop), Yampolsky became interested in photography. [7] At first, she only took pictures for Taller de Gráfica Popular. [8] Then she decided to study photography at the San Carlos Academy. [9] In the late 1960s, she traveled around Mexico for three years and took pictures of everyday life. [10] Yampolsky lived and worked in Mexico for the rest of her life. [11] While she living in Mexico, Yampolsky took more than 66,000 photographs.

Grammar Forms

6.1 Past Progressive

Subject	Verb	Example
I / he / she / it	*was* (*not*) + verb + *-ing*	In 1910, artist Pierre Bonnard **was living** in Paris when he decided to move to the south of France.
you / we / they	*were* (*not*) + verb + *-ing*	As the actors **were leaving** the stage, all of the lights went out.

Note
The past progressive is also referred to as the past continuous.

ACTIVITY 1

Fill in the blank with the correct past progressive form of the verb in parentheses. Use *not* when it is there.

1. When she lived in Portugal in the early 1990s, J. K. Rowling _____ (*teach*) English.

2. From 1909 to 1913, the American architect Frank Lloyd Wright _____ (*live*) in Germany.

3. In the 1960s, many African-Americans _____ (*fight*) for civil rights.

4. Barack Obama _____ (*work*) in poor neighborhoods of Chicago during the mid-1980s.

5. During the 2008 financial crisis, it was difficult for college graduates to find jobs because many industries _____ (*not, hire*) new employees.

6. Beatle John Lennon _____ (*tour*) Britain in 1963 when his son Julian was born.

7. Barbie dolls _____ (*not, sell*) well in China, so Mattel closed the Shanghai Barbie store.

8. When Mark Zuckerberg started Facebook, he _____ (*attend*) Harvard.

Common Uses

6.2   Using Past Progressive

The past progressive is used only in certain cases in academic writing:

1. to describe an action that was happening at a specific time in the past	 The economy **was showing** signs of failing in 2015.
2. to describe an action in the past that was interrupted • Use *when* + simple past for the interruption. • Use *while* or *as* + past progressive for the action in progress.	 The third game of the 1989 World Series **was** just **starting** when the earthquake **hit**. action in progress interruption As they **were approaching** the summit action in progress of Mt. Everest, Bishop and Jerstad **noticed** that their oxygen was low. interruption
3. to provide background or to set the scene in a narrative	It was an ordinary day at work for Percy Spencer. He **was working** at Raytheon. He and his colleagues **were doing** research on radar equipment when the candy bar in his pocket began to melt.

Note
Stative (nonactive) verbs are not usually used in the progressive. Stative verbs include *sound, smell, taste, feel, look, like, love, hate, want, need, know, seem, think, belong, include, have.*

Fill in the blank with the correct past or past progressive form of the verb in parentheses. In some cases, either form is correct.

1. In 2014, Apple _____ (*download*) a U2 album onto everyone's mobile devices, whether they wanted it or not.

2. Due to the Depression, 6 million Americans _____ (*look*) for work and not finding it in 1931.

3. About 75 homeless people _____ (*live*) in the New York Subway tunnels during the early 1990s.

4. Hiroshi Amano was traveling from Japan to Germany when he _____ (*hear*) that he won the 2014 Nobel Prize in physics.

5. More than half a billion people were watching TV when Neil Armstrong _____ (*step*) on the moon.

6. The Berlin Wall was about to come down. People _____ (*gather*) at the wall. They were chanting "*Tor auf!*" ("Open the gate!").

7. It was the summer of 1847. James Marshall was working at John Sutter's sawmill in California. Marshall _____ (*dig*) in a stream to create power for the mill. Suddenly, Marshall saw some shiny objects in the stream.

8. Naval engineer Richard James was working with springs when one of them _____ (*fall*) to the floor and kept bouncing from place to place. From this experience, he invented the popular Slinky toy in 1943.

Common Errors

Common Error 6.1   Do you have the correct past progressive form?

> was burning
> The fire ~~was burn~~ in the attic when the firefighters arrived.
>
> was teaching
> J. K. Rowling ~~teaching~~ English in Portugal when she started the first Harry Potter book.

REMEMBER: Form the past progressive with *was / were* (*not*) + verb + *-ing*.

ACTIVITY 3   **Common Error 6.1**

Check each sentence for the correct past progressive form. If the verb form is correct, write *C* on the line in front of the sentence. If it is incorrect, write *X* on the line and mark the correction.

_____ **1.** George Washington planning on going back to farming when the Constitutional Convention delegates asked him to run for president.

_____ **2.** Roald Dahl got the idea for his book *Over to You: 10 Stories of Flyers and Flying* while he was flying planes in the Royal Air Force.

_____ **3.** Some of the world's greatest scientists, such as Enrico Fermi and Robert Oppenheimer, doing atomic research during World War II.

_____ **4.** For thousands of years, Native Americans living on the Bering Land Bridge, which connected Asia and North America.

_____ **5.** Thomas Hunt Morgan was teaching at Columbia University when he started experimenting on fruit flies.

_____ **6.** Conservationist Gary Roberts flying near the Cameroon border when he saw 15 to 20 dead elephants in the fields below.

_____ **7.** Roberts learned that ivory hunters were using rifles and grenades to kill elephants in Cameroon's Bouba Ndjida National Park.

_____ **8.** While the students reading, the researchers recorded their eye movements.

_____ **9.** The Golden State Warriors basketball team was play its first game of the playoff series when Stephen Curry injured his ankle.

_____ **10.** Even though Curry kept playing, it was clear to the crowd that he feeling some pain.

Common Error 6.2　Do you need simple past or past progressive?

> *were testing*
> Astronauts Virgil "Gus" Grissom, Edward H. White, and Roger Chaffee ~~tested~~ the spacecraft when a fire started in the cabin.

REMEMBER: Use past progressive to emphasize an action that was in progress. Use past tense for the action that interrupted it.

ACTIVITY 4　**Common Error 6.2**

Fill in the blank with the correct past or past progressive form of the verb in parentheses.

1. In 1929, Andrew Irvine and George Mallory _____ (*climb*) Mount Everest when they _____ (*disappear*).

2. Frank Abagnale _____ (*pretend*) to be other people—such as an airline pilot and a doctor—for years until the police finally _____ (*catch*) him in 1969.

3. When he _____ (*form*) his first band, American jazz composer and bandleader Duke Ellington _____ (*live*) in Washington, D.C.

4. The crew and passengers of US Airways Flight 1549 _____ (*fly*) over the Hudson River when a flock of Canadian geese _____ (*fly*) into the plane's engines.

5. While he _____ (*study*) at the Tisch School of the Arts, director Ang Lee _____ (*make*) his first film, *Shades of the Lake*.

6. Queen Elizabeth II _____ (*visit*) Kenya when she _____ (*learn*) that her father, King George VI, was dead.

7. Benjamin Franklin _____ (*fly*) a kite in a storm when lightning _____ (hit) a key attached to the kite string.

8. While he _____ (*serve*) time in Robben Island Prison, Nelson Mandela _____ (*write*) a 500-page autobiography.

Academic Vocabulary

attend	learn	read	teach	use
do	make	take	try	work

Source: Corpus of Contemporary American English (Davies 2008–)

ACTIVITY 5   **Vocabulary in Academic Writing**

Use the past progressive form of the academic vocabulary to complete the sentences. Use *not* when it is there. For some sentences, more than one answer is possible.

Subject Area   **Example from Academic Writing**

Criminal Justice

1. While the sheriff _____ a routine investigation, the suspect made a confession.

Environmental Science

2. Several workers became ill while they

_____ dangerous cleaning products.

Psychology

3. While the students _____ a list of new words, the researchers played classical music.

American Literature

4. William Carlos Williams published his first book of poems while he

_____ as a doctor.

English Composition

5. Hanan Al Hroub won the Global Teacher Prize while she

_____ at the Samiha Khalil Secondary

School in Palestine.

History

6. While President Obama _____ to give a speech at the White House in 2015, a protester interrupted him several times.

Media Studies

7. While Francis Ford Coppola _____ the movie *Apocalypse Now,* the actor Martin Sheen had a heart attack.

Education

8. Many students became nervous while they

_____ the test, and 20 percent did not

finish it.

Counseling

9. The students who had the highest grade point averages

_____ universities that offered free

counseling services.

Communication

10. Many people agreed that President Clinton _____ (*not*) his notes when he gave a speech at the 2012 Democratic convention.

Put It Together

Multiple Choice Choose the letter of the correct answer.

1. The famous scientist Alexander Fleming accidentally discovered penicillin when he _____ something else.

   a. studying   **b.** was studying   **c.** were studying   **d.** studied

2. The first *Star Wars* movie _____ in 1977.

   a. was appearing   **b.** appear   **c.** appeared   **d.** appearing

3. Che Guevara took notes on his experiences while he _____ around South America.

   a. travels   **b.** was traveling   **c.** traveling   **d.** were traveling

4. The Giants and the Athletics _____ the third game of the 1989 World Series when the Loma Prieta earthquake hit the San Francisco Bay area.

   a. played   **b.** playing   **c.** were playing   **d.** play

5. Percy Spencer was working at Raytheon when he _____ that microwaves can cook food.

   a. discovered   **b.** was discovering   **c.** discovering   **d.** discovers

Error Correction One of the five underlined words or phrases is not correct. Find the error and correct it. Be prepared to explain your answer.

6. Before he came to the United States, Ha Jin studying at Heilongjiang University in China.

7. Most of the participants were still working on the test when the researcher asks them to stop.

8. By 2014, most American adult were using cell phones for the majority of their phone calls.

Paul Nicklen, National Geographic Explorer and Photographer, gets a close view of a leopard seal in Antarctica.

ACTIVITY 7 **Building Greater Sentences**

Combine these short sentences into one sentence. You can add new words and move words around, but you should not add or omit any ideas. More than one answer is possible, but these sentences require the past progressive.

1. **a.** Paul Nicklen is a wildlife photographer.
   b. He was photographing a leopard seal.
   c. At the same time, the seal swam close to Nicklen.
   d. The seal opened her mouth.
   e. She put Nicklen's camera into her mouth.

2. **a.** Steve Wozniak was attending the University of California at Berkeley.
   b. During this time, he met Steve Jobs.
   c. They started working together.

3. **a.** The researcher played Mozart.
   b. At the same time, students were taking a test.
   c. The reason was that the researcher wanted to show something.
   d. Listening to music helps people concentrate.

Read the paragraph. Then follow the directions in the 10 steps below to edit the information and composition of this paragraph. Write your revised paragraph on a separate sheet of paper. Be careful with capitalization and punctuation. Check your answers with the class.

NARRATIVE PARAGRAPH

The First and Last Trip of the *Titanic*

[1] On April 10, 1912, the RMS *Titanic* left England for the United States. [2] It was the largest passenger ship ever built. [3] It was so big and so safe that people called it "unsinkable." [4] The ship was carrying a total of 2,240 passengers. [5] At around 11:30 p.m. on the fourth night of the trip, the *Titanic* was sailing in calm water under a clear sky. [6] Most of the passengers were sleeping. [7] The ship was moving at full speed. [8] Suddenly one of the ship's crewmembers, Frederick Fleet, saw an iceberg. [9] The ship was heading directly toward it. [10] Fleet rang a bell and called the captain. [11] The captain tried to turn the ship to avoid the iceberg, but it was too late. [12] The *Titanic* turned. [13] It hit the iceberg while it was turning. [14] The ship began to sink. [15] By the next morning, the ship was underwater. [16] More than 1,550 people died in the disaster, and close to 700 people survived. [17] They are all gone now, but some remaining parts of the *Titanic* are still lying at the bottom of the ocean today.

---

1. Combine sentences 1 and 2. Delete *It was* and put the rest of sentence 2 between *the RMS Titanic* and *left for England*. Remember to put commas around the phrase.

2. In sentence 3, change *It* to *The Titanic* to be clearer and to avoid using *it* again.

3. In sentence 4, give specific details about the passengers to make the narrative more interesting. (Hint: The passengers were a combination of wealthy people and immigrants on their way to America.)

4. Combine sentences 5 and 6 with *and*

5. Combine sentences 7 and 8 with *when*.

6. Sentences 12, 13, and 14 are short and choppy. Combine them into one sentence. (Hint: Use the verb *turn* only once, in the past progressive. Use *and* to add sentence 14.

7. In sentence 15, add the exact time and date after *By*. Details make a narrative more interesting. (Hint: The event happened at 2 a.m. on April 15th.)

8. In sentence 15, replace *the ship* with *the Titanic* to avoid repetition.

9. In sentence 15, add the intensifier *completely* to add drama to the narrative. (Hint: It is an adverb, so it goes after the main verb in the sentence.)

10. In sentence 17, replace *some remaining parts of the Titanic* with *the remains*. It says the same thing without using too many words.

ACTIVITY 9   Original Writing

On a separate sheet of paper, write a narrative paragraph (at least five sentences) about an event that interests you. Use at least two examples with past progressive and underline them.

Here are some examples of how to begin.

- *The discovery of DNA was one of the most important scientific breakthroughs of all time.*
- *The most exciting soccer game the world has even seen was the Liverpool-Alaves match in 2001.*
- *October 17, 1989, began as an ordinary day for most Northern Californians.*

A French project manager works on software to help doctors diagnose eye problems in patients.

7 Writing about the Future

WHAT DO YOU KNOW?

DISCUSS Look at the photo and read the caption. Discuss the questions.

1. The man in the photo is an software engineer. How will his work help patients?

2. How is technology changing how doctors and patients can interact?

FIND THE ERRORS This paragraph contains two errors with verbs in the future. Find the errors and correct them. Explain your corrections to a partner.

DESCRIPTIVE PARAGRAPH

Doctors' Appointments in the Future

[1] In the future, the way people receive health care from their doctor is going to be different than it is now. [2] For instance, they may have online video appointments with their doctor and not go to a doctor's office for a physical examination. [3] In the future, when people feel sick, they will go to a pharmacy first, buy a test, and get an instant diagnosis. [4] Then they will to talk to their doctor about it online to receive a treatment plan. [5] People will probably wear a health tracker that collects biodata, and that data will be sent to the doctor. [6] They will not need to schedule a follow-up appointment. [7] For some diseases, the doctor may assign them to a group where several patients with the same illness will share information electronically, and the doctor will gives them individual or group advice.

Grammar Forms

7.1	Future with *Will* or *May*	
Subject	**Verb**	**Example**
I / you / he / she / it we / they	*will* + verb *will* + *not* + verb	The oceans **will rise** if polar ice melts. Someday, cars **will not use** gasoline.
I / you / he / she / it we / they	*may* + verb *may* + *not* + verb	In the future, people **may live** on the moon. Global warming **may not continue** past 2050.

Notes

1. Contractions are informal and are almost never used in academic writing. For the negative, use either *will not* + verb or *will* + verb + *no* + noun.

   In a few years, there **will not be** any elephants.

   In a few years, there **will be no** elephants.

2. Adverbs (*probably, certainly, likely, never,* etc.) are placed between *will* and the base verb.

   After the pollution is gone, fish **will likely return** to the river.

3. Words that show a future time (*soon, in a few years, next week, when*) can be at the beginning or end of the sentence.

   The forest will be gone **in a few years**.

   In a few years, there will be no trees here.

7.2	Future with *Be Going To*	
Subject	**Verb**	**Example**
I	*am* + (*not*) *going to* + verb	In this paper, I **am going to explain** the advantages and disadvantages of taking night classes. I **am not going to make** a decision until I see more evidence.
you / we / they	*are* + (*not*) *going to* + verb	In the future, more people **are going to grow** their own food. The nurses **are not going to return** to work until their demands are met.
he / she / it	*is* + (*not*) *going to* + verb	In the next decade, the cost of a college education **is going to increase**. The cost of laptops **is not going to increase** in the near future.

Fill in the blank with the correct form of the future time verb in parentheses. Use *not* or *no* when it is there.

1. In this paper, I _____ (*will, explain*) the benefits of buying food from small farms.

2. In this paper, I _____ (*be going to, explain*) the problems with large food producers.

3. Someday, personal robots for both children and adults _____ (*will, be*) in every home.

4. Personal robots _____ (*be going to, be*) available for children in the near future.

5. Some manufacturers hope that hydrogen _____ (*will, replace*) gasoline as fuel for cars.

6. There are already signs that an automotive company _____ (*be going to, manufacture*) alternative-fuel taxi cabs.

7. A few inventors think that the old-fashioned steam engine _____ (*may, replace*) the gasoline engine.

8. Because of human beliefs, science _____ (*not, will, solve*) all of mankind's problems.

9. Science _____ (*not, be going to, solve*) all of mankind's problems.

10. Families of cancer victims dream of the day when there _____ (*no, will, be*) cancer in the world.

Common Uses

7.3	Using Verbs with Future Time
1. Use *will* + verb for a future action that you are certain of or for a prediction. • Use for the introduction or conclusion of a paper.	In this paper, I **will explain** . . . This report **will describe** . . . Some scientists say that the Amazon rainforest **will not survive** for future generations.
2. Use *will* + *probably* + verb for a future action that you are less certain of.	The dentist **will probably want** to see X-rays.
3. Use *may* + verb to express a future possibility.	Numerous reports indicate that Mt. Fuji **may erupt** again.
4. Use *be going to* + verb for future plans that you are very certain of. • *Be going to* is almost never used in academic writing. This verb structure is more common in conversation. However, it is possible to use *be going to* in an introduction.	This paper **is going to explain** a construction method for earthquake-safe buildings.

Note

In academic writing, *may* + verb is more common than *will* + verb because writers are often not completely certain.

ACTIVITY 2

In each sentence, underline the future form, including the base verb. Then underline the word(s) in parentheses that tell the use of the verb.

1. (*possibility / certain*) This report will describe the behaviors of preschool children during story time.

2. (*possibility / certain*) Although a volcano has not erupted in Argentina for almost 200 years, reports indicate that one may erupt in the near future.

3. (*possibility / a plan*) In order to have better crops, farmers in Senegal are going to use a new machine from India to plant seeds next year.

4. (*less certain / certain*) It is predicted that cars of the future will not need a driver.

5. (*less certain / a plan*) Once a wolf kills a lamb, it will probably return to the flock for more.

6. (*less certain / a plan*) A person who buys stock in a company believes that the price of that stock is going to increase.

7. (*possibility / less certain*) One day a college education may be free for everyone.

8. (*possibility / certain*) Requiring students to wear school uniforms will not stop all forms of bullying.

Common Errors

Common Error 7.1 Do you have the correct form with *will* or *may?*

will begin
The research ~~will to begin~~ in August.

find
New nurses may ~~finding~~ night shifts difficult.

may be
Tomorrow's energy source ~~maybe~~ from the sun.

REMEMBER: • Use the base verb only. Do not use *to* with the base verb after *will* or *may*.
 • Do not add *-ed* or *-ing* to the end of the verb.
 • *May + be* is a verb that follows the subject. *She may be sick.*
  Maybe is an adverb that often begins a sentence. *Maybe she is sick.*

ACTIVITY 3 **Common Error 7.1**

In each sentence, underline the future verb. If the verb form is correct, write *C* on the line. If it is wrong, write *X* on the line. Then write the correct word above the incorrect word in the sentence.

_____ **1.** According to the World Health Organization, eating processed meats maybe cause cancer.

_____ **2.** Many people worry that they will not have enough money to live well after they retire.

_____ **3.** Although building a new dam will to create necessary electricity, it may eventually hurt the fish population in the river.

_____ **4.** An electrical resistor is anything that will reduced the amount of electricity that flows through it.

_____ **5.** Houses in the future will probably have rooftop gardens.

_____ **6.** Tourists to Campeche, Mexico, will seeing beautiful tropical flowers, Spanish architecture, and Mayan ruins.

_____ **7.** Archaeologists may never discover the origin of the statues on Easter Island.

_____ **8.** Bioengineers are trying to create living cells that will heal diseases.

Common Error 7.2   Do you have the correct future form?

>   *to*
> This town is going ∧ build three new schools.

REMEMBER: For future, use *be going to* + verb *or will / may* + verb.

ACTIVITY 4   **Common Error 7.2**

For each pair of sentences, underline the correct verbs in the parentheses. Both the simple present and simple future are used.

1. A team from the university (*is going begin / is going to begin*) work on a search and rescue robot. They hope it (*will be / will is*) ready to use by next year.

2. In summary, this study suggests that Yoga exercise (*may help / is going help*) people sleep more soundly. Further research on sleep aids (*helps / will help*) support these claims.

3. Borrowing money (*may seems / may seem*) like an easy solution when you are unable to pay your bills. However, if you do not have a plan for how to balance your personal budget, you (*will probably need / will probably needing*) to keep borrowing money.

4. A soccer player with an injury (*maybe not able / may not be able*) to perform well, and the coach (*will likely keep / will likely to keep*) him out of the game.

Academic Vocabulary

Verbs Frequently Used with *May* in Academic Writing

be	have	include	need	result
find	help	lead	provide	seem

Source: Corpus of Contemporary American English (Davies 2008–)

ACTIVITY 5 **Vocabulary in Academic Writing**

Use the academic vocabulary with *may* to complete the sentences.

Subject Area	Example from Academic Writing
Sports Management	**1.** From time to time, players _____ injuries that prevent them from playing in a competition.
Computer Engineering	**2.** A demand for better wireless networks _____ in new technology being developed.
Nursing	**3.** In some communities, public health nurses _____ education to the citizens about infectious diseases.
Business Management	**4.** Even though spending money on environmental issues _____ like a loss of profits, many consumers will buy from corporations that support social responsibility.
Linguistics	**5.** Research shows that if young children experience two languages equally, they _____ bilingual at an early age.
Geology	**6.** In regions where there is no surface water, hydrogeologists _____ water deep below the surface within a layer of rocks.
Music	**7.** K-pop songs may sound like American pop music, but the musicians _____ sounds of traditional Korean music.
Climatology	**8.** With climate change, some plants will probably not survive and animals may die. Therefore, a major climate change _____ to some animals disappearing forever.
Education	**9.** Teaching reading strategies _____ students become better readers.
Engineering	**10.** As the world's population increases, engineers _____ to design cities under the sea.

Put It Together

ACTIVITY 6   Review Quiz

Multiple Choice   Choose the letter of the correct answer.

1. In the 1990s, most people bought music on cassettes, but audio cassette tapes _____ popular again.

    a. may never be   **b.** may being   **c.** maybe never   **d.** may never

2. The Canadian hockey team believes that they _____ the Olympic gold medal.

    a. be going to win   **b.** is going to win   **c.** going to win   **d.** d. are going to win

3. Unless researchers find a cure, the number of people with diabetes will not _____.

    a. decreasing   **b.** decreased   **c.** decrease   **d.** to decrease

4. A dog _____ at a stranger who knocks on the door.

    a. will likely bark   **b.** will bark likely   **c.** will likely barks   **d.** will likely barking

5. Because some plastics last for hundreds of years, future archaeologists _____ plastic fossils in the ground.

    a. may will   **b.** may find   **c.** will to find   **d.** may finds

Error Correction   One of the five underlined words or phrases is not correct. Find the error and correct it. Be prepared to explain your answer.

6. Incorrect food storage <u>may cause</u> food poisoning. <u>It</u> is safer to divide hot leftover food into several small <u>container</u> in the refrigerator because it <u>will take</u> longer <u>to cool</u> food in a large container.

7. Dolphins <u>usually work</u> together to eat. First, they <u>will find</u> a school of fish. <u>Next</u>, several of them <u>will</u> form a circle around the fish. Finally, one will <u>swims</u> into the circle to eat.

8. <u>At some point</u> during your college education, an <u>instructor is going ask</u> you to make a speech. The <u>most important</u> thing to remember is that you will <u>need</u> a topic that <u>will</u> interest the audience.

Flames from a massive forest fire in Washington state light up the night.

Building Greater Sentences

Combine these short sentences into one sentence. You can add new words and move words around, but you should not add or omit any ideas. More than one answer is possible, but these sentences require verb forms for future time.

1. a. Forest fires will increase.
   b. The fires are global.
   c. The increase is likely.
   d. This is because of climate change.

2. a. Computer engineers will need to develop security.
   b. The security will need to be better.
   c. This is because more information will be available.
   d. This information will be in the future.

3. a. A railway is going to connect China and Singapore.
   b. It will be high-speed.
   c. It will be in a few years.

Steps to Composing

Read the paragraph. Then follow the directions in the 10 steps below to edit the information and composition of this paragraph. Write your revised paragraph on a separate sheet of paper. Be careful with capitalization and punctuation. Check your answers with the class.

CAUSE–EFFECT PARAGRAPH

The Dangers of Plastic Garbage in the Oceans

[1] Plastic garbage floating in our oceans is a serious global problem that affects marine life and beaches. [2] First, injuries to marine life are far-reaching. [3] Birds and fish may think pieces of plastic are small fish and eat them. [4] The plastic may cause them to become very sick. [5] A turtle may swim into a plastic bag. [6] Furthermore, a dolphin or whale may get caught in nets and drown. [7] In addition to harming marine life, this garbage spoils the beaches. [8] It hurts tourism. [9] A recent study estimated that 8 million metric tons of plastic reaches the world's oceans every year, and this number may increase because of the growing population. [10] In conclusion, if we do nothing to stop this pollution, the problems may get worse.

---

1. To sentence 1, add *Tons of* before the word *plastic*.

2. Sentence 3 needs a better description of the plastic. Change *pieces of plastic* to *shiny pieces of broken plastic*.

3. Add another effect of eating plastic in sentence 4. After *very sick* add the words *or die*.

4. Add a clause to sentence 5: *and it may not be able to free itself*.

5. For sentence 6, make the subjects plural.

6. In sentence 7, add *plastic* to the word *garbage*.

7. Sentence 8 needs a reason. Add *because it is unattractive*.

8. More support is needed in the second part. After sentence 8, add a new sentence: *Additionally, someone may get hurt by stepping on something sharp*.

9. The study mentioned in sentence 9 shows the evidence about the future, which allows the writer to make a stronger statement about the future. In sentence *9*, change *may* to *will likely*.

10. The use of *may* in this conclusion sentence is weak. The writer gave evidence by mentioning the survey and the growing population. Change *may* to *are only going to* in sentence 10 to express a stronger opinion in the conclusion.

ACTIVITY 9 Original Writing

On a separate sheet of paper, write a cause-effect paragraph (at least five sentences) about something in the future. Use at least two examples of future time (*will, may*, or *be going to*). Underline your examples.

Here are some examples of how to begin.

- *Fifty years from now, cars/houses will have several new features to improve safety/ efficiency/ecological friendliness.*
- *Global climate changes may cause some animals to disappear forever.*
- *The best research for government to invest money in is new energy sources/space exploration/medical discoveries because that research will have several positive effects.*

Visitors dig for clams as they make their way across the land bridge that appears twice a year between two islands in South Korea.

8 Writing with Subject–Verb Agreement

WHAT DO YOU KNOW?

DISCUSS Look at the photo and read the caption. Discuss the questions.

1. Why is this a special event for the people in the photo?
2. What other special natural events do people enjoy watching?

FIND THE ERRORS This paragraph contains two errors with subject–verb agreement. Find the errors and correct them. Explain your corrections to a partner.

DESCRIPTIVE PARAGRAPH

The Amazing Jindo-Modo Land Bridge

¹Twice a year, something very interesting happens with the water of the Myeongyyang Strait in South Korea. ²Between the months of April and June, extremely low ocean tides occur between the islands of Jindo and Modo. ³When this happens, a land bridge that is 1.3 miles long appear between the two islands, and this allows the residents to walk from one island to the other. ⁴During this time, people dig for clams in the mud of the temporary path and visit with friends. ⁵However, this land remains dry for only one hour, so their time together is very short. ⁶High tide soon covers the path, and all the people in the area looks forward to the next time that they can walk on the bottom of the sea.

Grammar Forms

8.1　Subject–Verb Agreement

Subject	Verb	Example
I / you / we / they	verb	Penguins **live** on the southern half of the planet.
he / she / it	verb + -s	A penguin **spends** about half its life in water and half on land.

Notes

1. If a verb ends in consonant + -y, change the y to i and add -es.

    cry ⟶ cries   carry ⟶ carries

2. If a verb ends in -o, add -es.

    do ⟶ does   go ⟶ goes

8.2　Subject–Verb Agreement: Irregular Verbs

Subject	Verb	Example
be	I *am* I *was*	I **am** a twin. My teaching career began when I **was** only 20 years old.
	he / she / it *is* he / she / it *was*	Nepal **is** in Asia. The information **was** difficult to find.
	you / we / they *are* you / we / they *were*	Nepal and Vietnam **are** in Asia. Belarus and Ukraine **were** in the Soviet Union.
have	I / you / we / they *have*	Adult humans **have** 32 teeth.
	he / she / it *has*	An adult cat **has** 30 teeth.

ACTIVITY 1

Fill in the blank with the correct form of the verb in parentheses.

1. This science experiment _____ (*contain*) many steps.

2. Universities often _____ (*have*) a policy against smoking on campus.

3. Lagos and Cairo _____ (*be*) two of the largest capital cities in Africa.

4. Additionally, 67 moons _____ (*revolve*) around the planet Jupiter.

5. A bear _____ (*need*) to sleep during the cold winter months because there is very little food for it to eat.

6. The Statue of Liberty _____ (*hold*) a tablet in her left hand and a torch in her right.

7. In many small successful companies, the president personally _____ (*reply*) to any mail from dissatisfied customers.

8. From a business point of view, farmers _____ (*worry*) about the weather and insects after they plant their crops.

Florida farmers work to protect young tomato plants from freezing temperatures.

Common Uses

Using Subject–Verb Agreement

In every sentence, the subject and verb must agree. This means that a singular subject needs a singular verb and a plural subject needs a plural verb. Using correct subject–verb agreement is very important in academic writing.

1. a. A singular verb in simple present ends in -*s*.	Winter **lasts** a long time in Alaska.
b. For the negative, use *does* + *not* + verb.	A goldfish **does not require** much care.
c. Noncount nouns always use a singular verb.	<u>Pollution</u> **damages** the environment in significant ways.
d. A subject with the words *every* or *each* is singular.	<u>Every</u> survey participant **is going to receive** the same set of questions.
2. A gerund (verb + -*ing*) is always singular.	<u>Visiting</u> Norway **costs** a lot of money.
• In academic writing, it is very common to use a gerund as the subject of a sentence.	<u>Visiting</u> Norway and Sweden **costs** a lot of money.
3. A phrase or a clause between the subject and verb does not usually change subject–verb agreement.	The <u>reason</u> for these recent changes **is** difficult to explain.
	The <u>reasons</u> for these recent changes **are** difficult to explain.
	A <u>player</u> who has more than 30 points **plays** a second time.
	<u>Players</u> who have a high score **play** a second time.
4. In *there* sentences, the subject comes after the verb. The verb must agree with the subject.	**There is** a <u>problem</u> with the new plan.
	There are three <u>reasons</u> for this decision.
• The word *there* is not a subject.	**There was** no <u>evidence</u> of cheating.
	There were five <u>speakers</u> at the conference.

5. A compound subject uses a plural verb.	The words *fiesta* and *siesta* **come** from Spanish, but they are common in English now.
6. A modal and its verb never change for singular or plural. • Modals include *can, will, should, may, must, might.*	A job interview **should last** about 30 minutes. Printers **can break** for many reasons.

ACTIVITY 2

Fill in the blank with the correct form of the verb in parentheses.

1. Hawaii and Mexico _____ (*export*) papayas.

2. Experts believe that certain types of music _____ (*increase*) a person's ability to concentrate on a task.

3. Lava _____ (*flow*) from Guatemala's Fuego volcano on a regular basis.

4. There _____ (*be*) a very thin line between success and failure.

5. Running a business _____ (*can*) require a significant amount of time and effort.

6. Every animal _____ (*have*) a scientific name and classification.

7. *One Hundred Years of Solitude* _____ (*be*) a novel by the famous Colombian author Gabriel García Márquez.

8. The problems that seem to be the most difficult often _____ (*have*) the easiest solutions.

9. Math homework _____ (*help*) students strengthen new skills that they learn in school.

10. Going from 0 to 62 miles per hour (100 kph) in two seconds _____ (*explain*) the thrill of professional car racing.

Common Errors

Common Error 8.1   Is the verb form correct?

control

Traffic lights ~~controls~~ the flow of automobiles during rush hour.

was

The candidate ~~were~~ presenting her points very effectively.

breaks

Glass ~~break~~ very easily.

requires

Swimming competitively ~~require~~ a great deal of determination.

REMEMBER: A subject and verb must agree in number (singular or plural). Noncount nouns and gerunds require singular verbs.

ACTIVITY 3   **Common Error 8.1**

In each set of sentences, use the words in parentheses to fill in the blanks with the correct form for subject–verb agreement. Use *not* when it is there.

1. Last year, investors _____ (*be*) planning to build a new shopping mall north of

the town. However, _____ (*there, be*) several problems with the location, so they

canceled the project.

2. Alaska and the mainland of the United States _____

(*not, share*) a common border. Every driver who wants to drive from Washington to Alaska

_____ (*must, cross*) into Canada and then _____ (*have*) to

drive for 37 hours to reach the Alaskan border.

3. Alligators and crocodiles _____ (*appear*) quite similar. However,

_____ (*there, be*) significant differences between the two animals. For

example, alligators _____ (*have*) U-shaped noses, but the nose of a crocodile

_____ (*be*) V-shaped. Additionally, only the crocodile _____

(*be*) able to lift its body completely off the ground.

4. In the U.S. legal system, judges _____ (*not, create*) laws. Instead, a judge _____ (*interpret*) laws and _____ (*use*) them to make decisions in court.

5. Many people _____ (*believe*) that the Sydney Opera House _____ (*be*) one giant building, but it actually _____ (*contain*) eight smaller performance areas. This amazing building _____ (*can, hold*) 5,700 people at one time.

6. American football players _____ (*must, wear*) a lot of protective equipment. However, in the equally violent sport of rugby, players _____ (*not, wear*) much protective equipment.

7. In the United States, voting for a new president and other high officials _____ (*be*) traditionally on the first Tuesday in November. The newly elected officials then _____ (*take*) office in January.

8. The process is relatively simple. When the metal _____ (*reach*) 2,500 degrees Fahrenheit, it _____ (*become*) a liquid. Then workers _____ (*pour*) it into a mold.

Molten metal is poured in a steel factory.

Common Error 8.2 Does the verb agree with the subject?

is

The <u>purpose</u> of the lessons <s>are</s> to teach the police dog to open the door.

seem

<u>Animals</u> that perform in a theme park sometimes <s>seems</s> depressed.

REMEMBER: • A noun after a preposition cannot be the subject. Look for the noun before the preposition.

  • A subject can be followed by an adjective clause. This clause gives more information about the subject. An adjective clause often starts with *who, that,* or *which.* The noun before the clause is the subject.

ACTIVITY 4 Common Error 8.2

Underline the subject. Then fill in the blank with the correct form of the verb or modal in parentheses. Use *not* when it is there.

1. According to a recent report, one of the most popular college majors

_____ (*be*) nursing.

2. For health reasons, a patient with a history of diabetes _____

(*should, meet*) regularly with a doctor.

3. During the winter months in Japan, groups of snow monkeys

_____ (*spend*) a great deal of time in hot springs.

4. Each year the overall winner of the Tour de France cycling race

_____ (*receive*) about $576,000.

5. Until 1950, the two tallest buildings in the world _____ (*be*)

the Empire State Building in New York and the Eiffel Tower in Paris.

6. Plants that grow in the desert _____ (*not, need*) very much

water to live.

7. The record for most tennis games in a tiebreaker at Wimbledon

_____ (*be*) still 70-68. John Isner and Nicolas Mahut set this

record in 2010.

8. A job candidate who has strong technology skills _____ (*have*)

an advantage over others.

Academic Vocabulary

Verbs from the Academic Word List (Sublist 1)

assume	distribute	function	involve	require
create	estimate	indicate	occur	vary

Source: Academic Word List (Coxhead 2000)

ACTIVITY 5   **Vocabulary in Academic Writing**

Use the correct form of the academic vocabulary to complete the sentences.

Subject Area	Example from Academic Writing
Astronomy	1. During a solar eclipse, the moon comes between the earth and the sun, and its shadow blocks the sun's light. Solar eclipses usually _____ twice a year.
Medicine	2. The amount of time that doctors spend with patients _____ greatly.
Biology	3. Experts agree that the average adult _____ approximately seven to nine hours of sleep a night.
Mechanical Engineering	4. Security is very important. In fact, the equipment only _____ properly after the user enters a secure password.
Political Science	5. Many voters _____ that most politicians are not completely truthful when they make promises to voters.
Architecture	6. All signs _____ that work on Antonio Gaudí's Cathedral of the Holy Family in Barcelona will be finished by 2026. This will be approximately 140 years after work on the building first began.
Sports Medicine	7. Recovering from an injury _____ both the athlete and the trainer.
Public Health	8. There are many ways to fight disease-carrying mosquitoes. For example, some governments in developing nations _____ free mosquito netting to their citizens.
Art	9. The artist Dale Chihuly _____ enormous sculptures using only glass.
Anthropology	10. Based on the most recent numbers, researchers _____ that the world's population will reach 9.6 billion by the year 2050.

Put It Together

Multiple Choice Choose the letter of the correct answer.

1. The paintings of the painter Georgia O'Keefe frequently _____ bright gigantic flowers.

   a. features   **b.** feature   **c.** is featuring   **d.** are featuring

2. Whales _____ the largest brains of any animal on the planet, and they can live for more than 60 years.

   a. possesses   **b.** possess   **c.** is possessing   **d.** are possessing

3. States often _____ tax benefits to encourage film companies to film in their cities.

   a. is creating   **b.** are creating   **c.** creates   **d.** create

4. There _____ many benefits to earning a college degree.

   a. is   **b.** are   **c.** does   **d.** do

5. Doing several exercises every morning _____ you lose weight.

   a. helps   **b.** help   **c.** is   **d.** are

Error Correction One of the five underlined words or phrases is not correct. Find the error and correct it. Be prepared to explain your answer.

6. During a leap year, Western calendars add one day to February, but the traditional Chinese calendar add an entire month every three years.

7. After a volunteer rescues an injured bird, he or she must cleans the oil from the bird's entire body with a gentle soap and water mixture.

8. There are no substitute for hard work and dedication when it comes to completing your college career.

Fruit bats fly in the early evening at Kasanka National Park, Zambia. These bats are part of a colony of about 8 million bats.

Building Greater Sentences

Combine these short sentences into one sentence. You can add new words and move words around, but you should not add or omit any ideas. More than one answer is possible, but all of these sentences require forms for subject–verb agreement.

1. **a.** Bats consume insects.
   b. Bats eat almost 3,000 insects.
   c. Bats do this in one night.

   _____

   _____

2. **a.** There are five volcanoes.
   b. These volcanoes are in the world.
   c. Only these contain lava lakes.

   _____

   _____

3. **a.** Gymnastics is a sport.
   b. Soccer is a sport.
   c. Both are popular sports.
   d. Both are Olympic sports.

   _____

   _____

Read the paragraph. Then follow the directions in the 10 steps to edit the information and composition of this paragraph. Write your revised paragraph on a separate sheet of paper. Be careful with capitalization and punctuation. Check your answers with the class.

DESCRIPTIVE PARAGRAPH

Animal Communication

[1] Animals do not use words. [2] Animals can communicate. [3] One way that animals are able to communicate is by making sounds. [4] For example, cats purr when they are happy, but they hiss to show anger. [5] Many types of insects rub their wings or legs together to send information. [6] Other animals use body language to communicate. [7] A dog uses its tail to transmit many messages. [8] A tail wag can mean that the animal is happy or scared. [9] Some animals communicate using odors. [10] Bears will rub against a tree to mark their personal areas. [11] Bees release a body chemical to warn other bees about danger. [12] Although animals do not have the ability to use words, they can most certainly express themselves.

---

1. Combine sentences 1 and 2 with the word *but*. Use a pronoun to avoid repeating the noun *animals*. Add correct punctuation.

2. In sentence 3, change *animals* to *animal* and make other necessary changes.

3. In sentence 4, change *cats* to *cat* and make other necessary changes.

4. In sentence 6, add the word *also* before the verb to mark the second major supporting sentence.

5. In sentence 7, change *dog* to *dogs* and make other necessary changes.

6. In sentence 8, add the adjective *angry* near the end of the sentence.

7. In sentence 9, add *Finally,* to the beginning of the sentence to mark the last major supporting sentence. Be sure to include the comma after this connecting word.

8. In sentence 11, change the subject *bees* to *bee* and make other necessary changes.

9. Combine sentences 10 and 11 with the word *and*.

10. In sentence 12, change the noun phrase *the ability* to the adjective *unable* and make other necessary changes, including the verb.

ACTIVITY 9 **Original Writing**

On a separate sheet of paper, write a descriptive paragraph (at least five sentences). Describe something or describe how a thing works. Make sure you use correct subject–verb agreement. Circle each subject and underline its verb.

Here are some examples of how to begin.

- *An elevator works by following a very specific process.*
- *A day in the life of a kindergarten teacher is not easy.*
- *A butterfly has a very interesting life cycle.*

Steve Jobs, chairman of Apple, stands in a room full of Apple computers in 1984.

9 Writing with Prepositions and Prepositional Phrases

WHAT DO YOU KNOW?

DISCUSS Look at the photo and read the caption. Discuss the questions.

1. What do you know about the Apple company?

2. How do the early computers look different from today's computers?

FIND THE ERRORS This paragraph contains two errors with prepositions. Find the errors and correct them. Explain your corrections to a partner.

NARRATIVE PARAGRAPH (BIOGRAPHY)

Steve Jobs

[1] Every person who uses a smart phone should thank Steve Jobs because his company helped advance the smart phone technology that all of us use today. [2] However, his involvement with technology began many years before. [3] In 1976, Jobs cofounded the internationally famous Apple company. [4] This company launched the Macintosh computer in 1984, which many believe was the beginning of today's desktop computers. [5] In 1985, Jobs left Apple and started a new company. [6] In 1997, Apple bought this new company, and Jobs was once again the head of Apple. [7] Financially, Steve Jobs was one of the most successful people in the tech field. [8] According in news reports, he was worth more than $100 million at age 25. [9] In October 5, 2011, Steve Jobs died at the age of 56. [10] He was one of the most important people of our time, and he will always be remembered for changing the way we communicate in our daily lives.

Grammar Forms

9.1 Single-word Prepositions

Prepositions	Examples
about	This essay talks **about** the lives of two politicians.
after	A tsunami may occur **after** an earthquake.
at	The White House is **at** 1600 Pennsylvania Avenue.
before	**Before** 1950, no one had a color TV.
for	One possible reason **for** the accident was bad weather.
from	People **from** Greece are called Greeks.
in	The United Nations began with 51 countries **in** 1945.
of	The purpose **of** this essay is to explain how clouds make rain.
on	Iguassu Falls is **on** the border of Brazil and Argentina.
since	The United States and Japan have worked together **since** 1950.
to	The Great Wall of China goes from Lop Lake in the west **to** Dandong in the east.
with	The prime minister consulted **with** his advisors.
without	It is difficult to start a business **without** a great deal of money.

9.2 Multiword Prepositions

Prepositions	Examples
according to	**According to** the survey, 29 percent of families have no emergency savings.
because of	**Because of** the cold climate, very few people live in Alaska.
due to	**Due to** the extreme heat, the researchers had to return to the base.
instead of	During an appointment, most people prefer to see a doctor **instead of** a nurse.
next to	Living **next to** a major highway can be bad for a person's health.

9.3 Prepositional Phrases

1. A prepositional phrase consists of a preposition and its object.	
a. The object can be a noun or a pronoun.	A giraffe is an example **of an African animal**. | prepositional phrase |
b. The object can be a gerund (verb + *-ing*)	Many people are afraid **of making a speech in public**. | prepositional phrase |
2. Prepositional phrases can occur in the beginning, middle, or end of a sentence. In academic writing, a comma comes after a prepositional phrase at the beginning of the sentence.	**Before moving ahead with the plan,** we should look at alternatives.

3. In academic writing, it is common to have prepositional phrases describing the subject. A prepositional phrase between the subject and the verb does not affect the verb.	The reason **for this decision** is clear.
	      S V
	The reason **for these decisions** is clear.
	      S V

Note

The word *to* is a preposition when it is followed by a noun (*to the airport*), but it is part of the infinitive when there is a verb (*to go, to be, to use*).

ACTIVITY 1

In each sentence, underline the prepositional phrases. The number of prepositional phrases in each sentence is shown in parentheses.

1. Without vitamin C in one's daily diet, it is difficult for a person to remain in good health. (4)

2. Many of the patients who take aspirin every day for better heart health are not aware of the possible health risks. (3)

3. Participating in team sports teaches children to depend on teammates for help. (3)

4. Due to a number of government fees and other costs, airlines have raised the price of most tickets. (3)

5. For a variety of reasons, the first day at his new job was a disaster from the very beginning until closing time. (5)

6. Traveling from countries in South America to Asia requires a change of planes in one or more cities. (5)

7. Malay is an example of a language with no verb tenses, but it is also different from English in several other important ways. (4)

8. Being in a car accident at age 15 changed how I think about many things. (3)

Common Uses

9.4 | Using Prepositions: Function

Prepositions are used to clarify ideas or to express specific information. They are used:

1. to show a place	**in** China / **at** Apple / **at** the Jeddah airport
2. to show time	**at** 6:15 p.m. (*at* + time) **on** September 11, 2001 (*on* + day / date) **in** 1992 (*in* + season / month / year / decade)
3. to show direction or movement	**to** the moon
4. to show a logical relationship	**because of** the error / **instead of** returning it
5. to specify, describe, or qualify nouns	the house **near** the beach immigrants **from** the northern part of the country

9.5 | Using Adjective + Preposition Combinations

afraid of	Most people are extremely **afraid of** speaking in public.
aware of	Very few people are **aware of** this problem.
different from	Spanish is **different from** Portuguese.
famous for	Alaska is **famous for** its beautiful scenery.
important for	Without a doubt, vitamin D is **important for** your health.
interested in	Students who are **interested in** entering medical school should focus on biology and chemistry.
necessary for	For U.S. citizens, a visa is **necessary for** entry to China.
ready for	Many people are not **ready for** a natural disaster.
satisfied with	If customers are **satisfied with** the service at a business, that place will do well.
similar to	In terms of grammar and vocabulary, Spanish is **similar to** Italian.
tired of	Many shoppers are **tired of** paying a sales tax on groceries.
worried about	Some experts are **worried about** recent changes in the world's weather.

9.6	Using Verb + Preposition Combinations
agree with	Many people do not **agree with** the president's new tax plan.
depend on	Your electricity bill **depends on** how much electricity you use.
differ from	A short story **differs from** a novel in three important ways.
focus on	This paper will focus on the **causes of** the Civil War.
listen to	To learn a language well, you should **listen to** songs in that language.
look for	Police are **looking fo**r clues to help find the bank robbers.
wait for	After taking the medicine, you must **wait for** 30 minutes before eating.
worry about	People **worry about** many different kinds of things.

9.7	Using Noun + Preposition Combinations
the cause of	No one really knows the real **cause of** the president's death.
the difference between	Do you know **the difference between** a noun and a pronoun?
an example of	*Dictionary* is **an example of** a word with four syllables.
an increase in	In early 2016, there was **an increase in** the cost of mailing a letter in Canada.
a need for	There is **a** real **need for** political change in our country.
the number of	**The number of** monarch butterflies is decreasing.
the reason for	Scientists are studying **the reasons for** our odd weather conditions.
the relationship between	What is **the relationship between** pollution and climate change?

Note
See Appendix 5, Prepositions, page 211 for more prepositions and preposition combinations.

ACTIVITY 2

Fill in the blank with the correct preposition. Sometimes more than one answer may be possible.

1. Due _____ the high cost _____ gold, many people now buy silver jewelry.

2. One clear difference _____ English and Arabic is the writing system, but the sounds in Arabic are also different _____ the sounds in English.

3. According _____ a recent report, skin cancer is the most common form _____ cancer _____ the United States.

4. _____ the last decade _____ Beethoven's life, he was almost totally deaf.

5. Malaysian Airlines Flight 370 departed _____ Kuala Lumpur _____ March 8, 2014, but it never arrived _____ its destination.

6. The sport _____ basketball was created by James Naismith _____ Massachusetts _____ 1891, but it did not become an official Olympic event _____ 1936.

7. There are many different types _____ apples, but some are better _____ cooking and some are better _____ you to eat fresh.

8. While the average American has 10 days _____ annual paid vacation, almost one-fourth _____ people who work _____ U.S. companies receive no paid holidays.

9. Many tourists who travel _____ Switzerland _____ July are not ready _____ the warm weather because they are not aware _____ how warm summers there can be.

10. To get accurate test results, it is necessary _____ the technician to measure the amounts _____ the chemicals very carefully.

112 UNIT 9 Writing with Prepositions and Prepositional Phrases

Common Errors

Common Error 9.1   Do you have the correct preposition?

in
Barack Obama became president of the United States ~~on~~ 2009.

REMEMBER: Some combinations of prepositions and nouns should be learned together because those words occur together very frequently.

ACTIVITY 3   **Common Error 9.1**

Fill in the blank with the correct preposition. Sometimes more than one answer may be possible.

1. _____ many recent years, more babies were born _____ August than _____ any other month.

2. My great-grandfather was born _____ Turkey, but his family moved _____ Canada _____ 1924.

3. This presentation will explain three ways to prepare _____ your first job interview.

4. While Mexican Spanish may seem similar _____ Colombian Spanish, they differ greatly _____ each other in both pronunciation and vocabulary.

5. There is an urgent need _____ more primary care doctors in the United States.

Common Error 9.2   Do you have a gerund after a preposition?

taking
Some parents worry about ~~take~~ their young children to the beach.

REMEMBER: Use a gerund after a preposition.

ACTIVITY 4   **Common Error 9.2**

Fill in the blank with the correct form of the verb in parentheses.

1. Without a doubt, many consumers _____ (*be*) very interested in _____ (*buy*) a new car some day.

2. At the present time, the police are _____ (*focus*) on _____ (*maintain*) peace in the neighborhood.

3. For apartments near the university, the cost of _____ (*live*) in a two-bedroom apartment _____ (*range*) from $900 to $1,200 per month.

4. Why do some people _____ (*excel*) in _____ (*learn*) a new language while it _____ (*present*) so many difficulties for others?

5. If there _____ (*be*) a problem with _____ (*return*) an item at a store, you should ask to _____ (*speak*) with a manager.

6. In the next step, _____ (*cover*) the test tube immediately after _____ (*remove*) it from the heat.

Common Error 9.3   Is there an error with *for*?

to
Studying history is important ~~for~~ avoid repeating our previous mistakes.

for
It is important ~~to~~ parents to make sure their children have some free time every day.

REMEMBER: *Be* + adjective is often followed by an infinitive *to* + verb. However, if the adjective is followed by a noun, use *for* before the noun.

ACTIVITY 5   **Common Error 9.3**

Read each sentence. Find the error with *for*, and write the correction with *to* above the error.

1. When you are ready for begin your data search, do a quick Internet search for the top five sites for your topic.

2. For many beginning adult learners of Chinese, it is difficult for learn how to write.

3. Because there are thousands of different types of insects, it is almost impossible for anyone for list all of them in one document.

4. Words with multiple vowels are often difficult for spell correctly

5. For the second time this month, the judge was very disappointed for find out that the jury was once again unable to reach a decision in this important case.

6. It is always recommended for make an outline before you write an essay.

Academic Vocabulary

Adjective + Preposition Combinations Frequently Used in Academic Writing

aware of	different from	involved in	responsible for
concerned about	interested in	related to	similar to

Source: Corpus of Contemporary American English (Davies 2008–)

ACTIVITY 6 **Vocabulary in Academic Writing**

Choose the best word and add the correct preposition to complete the sentence.

Subject Area	Example from Academic Writing
Biology	**1.** A crocodile is (*concerned / different / responsible*) _____ an alligator in several ways.
Political Science	**2.** Today we know that President Richard Nixon was definitely (*interested / involved / related*) _____ the Watergate Scandal in the 1970s.
Linguistics	**3.** English is more closely (*concerned / interested / related*) _____ German than to Spanish.
History	**4.** The purpose of this paper is to explain who might have been (*different / interested / responsible*) _____ starting World War I.
Health	**5.** Few people are (*aware / concerned / different*) _____ the fact that there are eight different essential nutrients called vitamin B.
Economics	**6.** When inflation rises rapidly, people are (*concerned / involved / similar*) _____ the buying power of their money.
English Literature	**7.** People are (*concerned / interested / responsible*) _____ reading and studying the short stories of O. Henry because he is the master of the surprise ending.
History	**8.** Twenty countries and the United Nations were (*involved / related / similar*) _____ the Korean War in the 1950s.
Science	**9.** The transfer of pollen from one plant to another can occur in several ways, but in general, insects and animals are (*interested / responsible / similar*) _____ most pollination.
Education	**10.** Although the two experiments used very different types of language learners, the results of Johnson's 2011 study were very (*concerned / involved / similar*) _____ the results from her 2006 study.

ACTIVITY 7 **Review Quiz**

Multiple Choice Choose the letter of the correct answer.

1. Social media experts are having a difficult time explaining the sudden increase _____ the number of hits on this web site.

   a. by **b.** for **c.** in **d.** on

2. _____ this day in history, a devastating earthquake struck in Chile.

   a. At **b.** For **c.** In **d.** On

3. Dilma Rousseff became the first female president of Brazil _____ June 2011.

   a. at **b.** by **c.** in **d.** on

4. Whether the university increases the number of scholarships depends _____ the budget that the president approves.

   a. for **b.** of **c.** on **d.** to

5. For citizens of Malaysia and Thailand, a visa is necessary _____ China.

   a. to visit **b.** to a visitor **c.** for a visit **d.** for visit

Error Correction One of the five underlined words or phrases is not correct. Find the error and correct it. Be prepared to explain your answer.

6. Not many travelers are agree with Sky Airlines' recent decision to charge more for checked luggage.

7. Most people do not know who can lead us during this transition, but there is definite need for new leadership in our company.

8. Instead of pay the workers a higher salary, the company announced that it will increase the number of paid vacation days for everyone.

Indonesian fishermen whose boats were destroyed by the 2004 tsunami use donated boats.

| ACTIVITY 8 | **Building Greater Sentences** |

Combine these short sentences into one sentence. You can add new words and move words around, but you should not add or omit any ideas. More than one answer is possible, but these sentences require prepositional phrases.

1. a. This paper will focus on the effects of the tsunami.
   b. The effects were devastating.
   c. The tsunami happened in 2004.
   d. The tsunami happened in Thailand and Indonesia.
   e. The tsunami happened in Sri Lanka and India.

_____

_____

2. a. Spanish is an example.   **c.** It is a Romance language.
   b. It is an example of a language.   **d.** It does not have phrasal verbs.

_____

_____

3. a. Many workers are tired.
   b. They are tired of making low salaries.
   c. They are tired of working long hours.
   d. They are tired of paying high taxes.
   e. This was according to a recent newspaper report.

_____

_____

Read the paragraph. Then follow the directions in the 10 steps below to edit the information and composition of the paragraph. Write your revised paragraph on a separate sheet of paper. Be careful with capitalization and punctuation. Check your answers with the class.

NARRATIVE PARAGRAPH (BIOGRAPHY)

William Shakespeare

[1] William Shakespeare is very famous. [2] However, we know very little about William Shakespeare's early life. [3] Shakespeare was born in Stratford-on-Avon. [4] He grew up in a large family with two sisters and three brothers. [5] On November 28, 1582, William Shakespeare married Anne Hathaway. [6] He was 18 years old. [7] She was 26. [8] During his career, Shakespeare wrote 37 plays for a group. [9] Many people came to see his plays, including *Romeo and Juliet* and *Hamlet*. [10] Because he was successful in the theater, Shakespeare became a wealthy man.

---

1. Combine sentence 1 and sentence 2 using the connector *but*. Do not repeat the person's name.

2. In sentence 3, add the phrase *the small town of*.

3. In sentence 3, add information about Shakespeare's birth year. Add the phrase *in 1564* in the correct place. Usually place information comes before time information.

4. In sentence 4, the important point is that he grew up in a large family, so the number of brothers and sisters is not important. Use the word *siblings* instead of *brothers* and *sisters*. Change the number, too.

5. In this biography, the time information is mostly in years, not exact dates. Therefore, in sentence 5, there is no reason to include the exact date of the wedding, so delete *November 28*. Be careful with the preposition.

6. Sentences 6 and 7 are very short and repetitive. Combine them.

7. In sentence 8, add the phrase *at least* in the correct place and add the adjective *acting* to tell what kind of group it was. Make any other necessary changes.

8. In sentence 9, add the play *Macbeth* as the third play. Make any other necessary changes.

9. In sentence 10, change the word *because* to the preposition *due to* or *because of*. (They are synonyms.) Make any other necessary changes.

10. The paragraph needs an ending. Add a concluding sentence about when Shakespeare died. Use the Internet to find the correct year. Start your sentence with the phrase *After a very productive career*.

ACTIVITY 10   **Original Writing**

On a separate piece of paper, write a narrative paragraph (at least five sentences) about the life of a famous person. Use at least one example of a preposition + year, one example of a noun + preposition, and one example of an adjective + preposition. Underline your examples.

Here are some examples of how to begin.

- (Name of person) was (profession):
  Guadalupe Victoria was the first president of Mexico.

- Perhaps the most (adjective) (profession) of all time was (name of person):
  Perhaps the most famous boxer of all time was Muhammad Ali.

- It is difficult to believe how many things (person) accomplished in (his/her) life:
  It is difficult to believe how many things Sojourner Truth accomplished in her life.

A man picks berries he has grown in his community garden in Somerset, England.

10 Writing with Modals

WHAT DO YOU KNOW?

DISCUSS Look at the photo and read the caption. Discuss the questions.

1. What do you know about community gardens? If you are not familiar with them, what do you think they are?

2. What are the benefits of growing your own fruits and vegetables? In other words, why do people have gardens?

FIND THE ERRORS This paragraph contains two errors with modals. Find the errors and correct them. Explain your corrections to a partner.

> ### PROCESS PARAGRAPH
>
> **How to Start a Community Garden**
>
> [1] In order to have a successful community garden, the organizers must follow some important steps. [2] First, they need to find a master gardener who can answer questions about soil, water, insects, and seed varieties. [3] Second, they should selects a location that is convenient for the members. [4] The location must receive at least six hours of full sun each day, and it must have access to water. [5] Next, they need to negotiate a lease from the land owner. [6] After that, the organizers can write the rules. [7] They should decide the size of each member's area and the collection of fees. [8] The rules could also include information about sharing tools. [9] In addition, the organizers can involve volunteers in preparing the planting areas. [10] Finally, a system should be set up to allow members to communicate with each other. [11] If the organizers remember to follow these steps, their community garden must be successful.

Grammar Forms

10.1 Modals: *Can, Could, May, Should, Must, Have To*

Modal + Verb	Example
can + verb	A tiger **can swim** nearly six kilometers.
could + verb	In high school, Jesse Owens **could run** 100 yards in less than 10 seconds.
may + verb	Someday, people **may live** in man-made cities that float on the ocean.
should + verb	Parents **should read** to their children.
must + verb	Food service workers **must wash** their hands.
have to + verb	Children **have to attend** school.

Notes

1. *Have to* is a phrasal modal and includes *to*. Use *has to* with a singular subject.
2. *May + be* is a modal. *Maybe* is an adverb used at the beginning of a sentence. *Maybe* is more common in spoken English than in academic writing.

   Bull sharks **may be** more aggressive than great white sharks.

10.2 Modals: Negatives

Form	Example
could / may / should / must + *not* + verb	Children **should not have** energy drinks.
cannot + verb	Alligators **cannot walk** backward.
do / does / did + *not* + *have to* + verb	A billionaire **does not have to work**. Because of online news, we **do not have to buy** newspapers.

Note

Modal contractions are possible, but they are informal and are almost never used in academic writing.

Read each sentence. Find the modal and verb combinations. Write *M* above the modal and *V* above the verb.

1. Most vegetables need full sun to grow well, but lettuce can grow in part shade.

2. Because water is important for life, we should not pollute our rivers and lakes.

3. A child with a peanut allergy could have a serious reaction after eating a peanut butter cookie.

4. For food safety reasons, refrigerator temperatures must be at or below 41 degrees Fahrenheit.

5. Although penguins are classified as birds, they cannot fly.

6. In order to find ancient jewelry, archaeologists have to look through the dirt very carefully.

7. Recent studies show that young adults should get seven to nine hours of sleep per night.

8. A glider pilot has to use air currents to keep the glider in the air.

Most gliders have no engine, although some have small engines to extend a flight or even take off.

Common Uses

Modals are auxiliary (helping) verbs that change the meaning of other verbs. Modals can express ability, possibility, opinion, advice, expectation and necessity. They can also express less than 100 percent certainty.

Use	Example
1. *Can* is used for present ability.	The great snipe is a bird that **can fly** from Sweden to southern Africa in two days.
2. *May* is used for a. present possibility b. future possibility • *May* is especially useful in academic writing when the writer cannot promise the future truth of the statement.	 Cave paintings in Australia **may be** the oldest in the world. Vegetables that are sprayed with certain chemicals **may cause** cancer.
3. *Could* is used for a. past ability b. present or future possibility	 Mozart **could write** music at age four. A giant asteroid **could hit** Earth.
4. *Should* is used for a. giving advice (a suggestion) b. expressing expectation	 In hot weather, people **should drink** more water. The spaceship launch **should take** place next month.
5. *Must* is used for things that are absolutely necessary, such as laws, rules, or requirements.	Soccer goals **must be** 24 feet wide.
6. *Have to* is used for something necessary: a. rules and requirements b. obligations	 A frog **has to live** near water. Members **have to pay** monthly dues.

7. The negative forms of *must* and *have to* change the meanings:	
a. *Must not* means something is prohibited.	Audience members **must not cheer** or **yell** during the televised debate.
b. *Do/Does/Did not have to* means something is not necessary.	Florence Nightingale **did not have to work**, yet she wanted to be a nurse.
8. Modals are useful in a conclusion to make a suggestion or give advice.	Since we need more schools, we **should vote** for the new bond. (*suggestion, recommendation*)
	Since we need more schools, we **must vote** for the new bond. (*necessity, very strong advice*)
9. Modals are useful at the end of a survey or scientific research to show a future possibility.	The results of this survey **could be** very useful for planning future activities.
10. The modals *can*, *could*, *may*, and *should* are useful in opinion writing. They can help to make the writer sound more believable.	Eating fresh fruit for breakfast results in weight loss. (*not always true; not believable*)
	Eating fresh fruit for breakfast **may result** in weight loss. (*more believable*)

Notes

1. *Can* is the most frequently used modal in academic writing. *May* occurs more frequently than *could*. (Corpus of Contemporary American English (Davies 2008–)

2. *May* and *could* are both used to indicate future possibility. In most contexts, *may* is more certain than *could*. However, in the negative, *could not* means a past or present impossibility, but *may not* indicates it is uncertain.

They **could not complete** the report. (*past impossibility*)

They **may not complete** the report. (*uncertainty*)

For each sentence, underline the modal and verb. Then underline the words in parentheses that tell the use of the modal in the sentence.

1. Marketing experts think that a restaurant in a department store could attract more shoppers.

   (*future possibility* / *present ability*)

2. People who live in an earthquake zone should keep an emergency supply kit.

   (*requirement* / *advice*)

3. Until the Berlin Wall came down in 1989, East Germans could not travel freely.

   (*not necessary* / *no past ability*)

4. In the Arctic Ocean, whales sometimes have to break through the ice to breathe.

   (*requirement* / *present possibility*)

5. Psychologists know that our body language can show our emotions.

   (*present ability* / *future possibility*)

6. Once the security system is turned on, the user must not open the door.

   (*not necessary* / *prohibition*)

7. In order for a couple to get married in the United States, they must have a marriage license.

   (*law* / *ability*)

8. According to astronomers, Halley's comet should be visible from Earth in 2062.

   (*expectation* / *possibility*)

9. Without certain plants for food, many animals may not adapt to climate change.

   (*possibility* / *impossibility*)

10. Without oxygen, humans could not live on Mars.

    (*possibility* / *impossibility*)

Common Errors

Common Error 10.1   Is the form of the modal correct?

If you drive a car, you must ~~to~~ buy auto insurance.

drink
A camel can ~~drinking~~ 30 gallons of water.

should
Everyone ~~must should~~ use sunscreen.

should not
People ~~do not should~~ look directly at the sun.

REMEMBER: • Do not use _to_ after a modal.
  • Modals are followed by the base verb.
  • Do not use two modals together.
  • _Not_ goes between the modal and verb. For _have to_, use _do/does not have to_ + verb.

ACTIVITY 3   Common Error 10.1

Read each sentence. If the modal + verb form is correct, write _C_ on the line. If it is wrong, write _X_ on the line. Underline the error and write the correction above it.

_____ **1.** Without proper training, marathon runners probably not could complete the course.

_____ **2.** Many older people could should benefit from a yoga exercise program.

_____ **3.** Patients who are participating in this medical research must not take any additional medicine.

_____ **4.** For legal reasons, a coach have to provide safety equipment to the athletes.

_____ **5.** Because of their different chemistry, oil and water no can be mixed.

_____ **6.** For fog to form, cool air must moving over warmer water.

_____ **7.** If you drive in the snow, you should have an emergency kit in your car.

_____ **8.** The power of ocean waves can generates electricity.

_____ **9.** The giant humpback whales can to dive to great depths in the ocean.

_____ **10.** Recent research suggests that e-cigarettes maybe addictive.

Common Error 10.2   Do you need a modal?

can cause
Smoking ~~causes~~ ^heart disease.

REMEMBER: If something is not true all of the time, modals *can, could, and may* make your information sound more believable.

Common Error 10.3   Is it the correct modal?

must not
Visitors to the zoo ~~do not have to~~ feed the animals.

REMEMBER: *Have to* and *must* have different meanings in the negative.

ACTIVITY 4   **Common Errors 10.2 and 10.3**

For each set of sentences, underline the correct verbs in parentheses.

1. Taking five classes in college (*is / could be*) very difficult for students who have a young family or a job. Therefore, before selecting classes, students (*should think / could think*) carefully about their time commitments.

2. King Charles XIV of Sweden (*could not speak / cannot speak*) Swedish when he became king in 1810. This is because he (*was / may be*) from France and (*could speak / can speak*) only French.

3. Some libraries today have reading nets hanging from wall to wall. Children (*could lie / can lie*) on them while they read books, and parents (*could watch / can watch*) the children from below.

4. Tipping requirements vary by country. In Finland, there is a law against tipping. Therefore, customers in Finnish restaurants (*must not tip / do not have to tip*) their servers. In Japan, customers (*cannot tip / should not tip*) because it is impolite. However, in a few countries, such as Italy, customers (*do not have to tip / have to tip*), but they (*can / cannot*) if they want to.

5. In most states, people (*must drive / can drive*) when they are 16 years old. First, they (*have to pass / should pass*) a driving test to obtain a license.

Academic Vocabulary

Verbs Frequently Used with *Can* in Academic Writing

be	have	lead	provide	take
do	help	make	see	use

Source: Corpus of Contemporary American English (Davies 2008–)

ACTIVITY 5   **Vocabulary in Academic Writing**

Use the academic vocabulary with *can* to complete the sentences.

Subject Area	Example from Academic Writing
Sociology	**1.** By doing volunteer work, we _____ a difference in the lives of others.
Biology	**2.** Some birds, such as the crow, _____ sticks and rocks to acquire food in nature.
Nursing	**3.** Studies show that being overweight _____ to diabetes and heart problems.
Communication	**4.** Certainly, most global corporations _____ things to improve their image.
Linguistics	**5.** Acquiring correct pronunciation _____ difficult for adult second language learners.
Ecology	**6.** After a forest fire, it _____ years for the forest to return.
Earth Science	**7.** The waves and tides of the ocean _____ energy.
Astronomy	**8.** With more powerful telescopes, astronomers _____ the moons of Saturn.
Education	**9.** Small trips outside of the classroom _____ students learn about careers.
Health	**10.** Doctors believe that stress _____ a significant impact on an individual's health.

Put It Together

Multiple Choice Choose the letter of the correct answer.

1. A new manager _____ questions before making changes.

   a. shoulds ask   **b.** should asks   **c.** should ask   **d.** must should ask

2. A basic rule of chemistry says that fire _____ without oxygen.

   a. cannot exists   **b.** cannot exist   **c.** no can exist   **d.** does not can exist

3. Medical researchers are looking for a gene that someday _____ cancer.

   a. could prevents   **b.** could to prevent   **c.** could prevent   **d.** will could prevent

4. Water in a bathtub _____ deep for a young child to drown.

   a. does not have to be   **b.** no have to be   **c.** have not to be   **d.** does not have be

5. For legal reasons, nurses _____ personal photos of patients.

   a. not must take   **b.** must not take   **c.** not must takes   **d.** must not takes

Error Correction One of the five underlined words or phrases is not correct.
Find the error and correct it. Be prepared to explain your answer.

6. Because there <u>are</u> not enough research on the health <u>effects</u> of caffeine, children <u>should</u> not <u>drink</u>

   caffeinated <u>beverages</u>.

7. In order to receive oxygen, the great white shark <u>must to swim</u> with <u>its</u> mouth open, <u>and</u>

   it must <u>not stop</u> swimming or it <u>will die</u>.

8. Because of space telescopes, scientists <u>can see</u> distant stars that Galileo <u>could not saw</u>

   400 years ago. Additionally, astronomers <u>can take</u> photos of planets today, but Galileo

   <u>could only draw</u> pictures <u>with</u> a pencil and paper.

Steam rises from a hot spring in Yellowstone National Park in Wyoming.

ACTIVITY 7   **Building Greater Sentences**

Combine these short sentences into one sentence. You can add new words and move words around, but you should not add or omit any ideas. More than one answer is possible, but these sentences require modals (*can, could, should, must, may, have to*).

1. **a.** A volcano erupts.
   b. There is a volcano below Yellowstone National Park.
   c. There is a possibility of this in the near future.

   _____

   _____

2. **a.** People send text messages.
   b. They do this while driving a car.
   c. They are prohibited from doing this.

   _____

   _____

3. **a.** Some students wear uniforms.
   b. These uniforms are at some schools.
   c. This is advice.
   d. This is to prevent bullying.

   _____

   _____

Steps to Composing

Read the paragraph. Then follow the directions in the 10 steps to edit the information and composition of the paragraph. Write your revised paragraph on a separate sheet of paper. Be careful with capitalization and punctuation. Check your answers with the class.

CAUSE–EFFECT PARAGRAPH

Dangers of Medicines for Babies

[1] Common cold and cough medicines can be life threatening to a baby. [2] As a result, it is important for parents to be very careful when giving any kind of medicine to a baby. [3] One common drugstore medicine for a cold or fever is aspirin. [4] Aspirin can cause Reye's syndrome, which in turn can cause a baby's death. [5] Orange-flavored children's cold and cough medicines are also available at drugstores and some grocery stores, but these attractive medicines are not for children under the age of two. [6] They may cause a baby's heart rate to become very low and bring about unconsciousness. [7] Another danger is with honey. [8] Even though honey is a food, many adults and children use honey as a remedy for coughs, but it is very dangerous to a baby. [9] Honey can have bacteria that babies do not digest. [10] This can cause serious weakness and breathing problems. [11] For these reasons, parents need a doctor's advice before giving any medicine to a baby.

---

1. In sentence 2, use a modal. Change the main clause of sentence 2 by replacing *it is important for parents to* with *parents should,* which uses the modal for giving advice.

2. Add more descriptive details to sentence 3. After the word *for,* add *the aches and pains of.*

3. Connect sentence 3 and 4 with the word *but* to contrast the two ideas. Change the period to a comma, and use a lower-case *a* for *aspirin.*

4. In sentence 4, the phrase *can cause* is used twice. Replace the second one with *could lead to,* which shows future possibility.

5. In sentence 5, replace *not* with *never* to give a more specific meaning.

6. In sentence 6, the modal *may* means uncertainty. Change the modal so the verb shows ability.

7. In sentence 7, replace the verb *is* with modal + *occur*. Use the modal for ability.

8. Sentence 8 has a clause that begins with *it is very dangerous*. Include a modal by changing the clause after *but* to *parents should never give honey to a baby.*

9. In sentence 9, change the verb *do not digest* to use the modal that shows negative ability.

10. Change the conclusion sentence by using a modal. Replace *need* with *should* and add a verb that fits in this sentence.

ACTIVITY 9 **Original Writing**

On a separate sheet of paper, write a cause–effect paragraph (at least five sentences) about ability, advice, or setting rules. Use at least two examples of modals (*can, could, should, must, have to & may*). Underline your modal and verb examples.

Here are some examples of how to begin.

- *According to parenting experts, parents must set clear rules for their children.*
- *Children's team sports should/should not give trophies to the winning team for three important reasons.*
- *Learning music can help a child learn other subjects.*

A shop owner chops chili peppers in a market in Ho Chi Minh City, Vietnam.

11 Using Simple Sentences

DISCUSS Look at the photo and read the caption. Discuss the questions.

1. Which country do you think produces the most chili peppers?

2. What is your favorite spicy food?

FIND THE ERRORS This paragraph contains two errors with simple sentences. Find the errors and correct them. Explain your corrections to a partner.

DESCRIPTIVE PARAGRAPH

The Valuable and Spicy Chili Pepper

[1] In many regions of the world, people use chili peppers to add heat to different kinds of food. [2] There are thousands of types of chili peppers, but they all belong to the same five species. [3] These are *Capsicum annuum, Capsicum baccatum, Capsicum chinense, Capsicum frutescens,* and *Capsicum pubescens.* [4] Where did chili peppers originate? Chili peppers originated in Mexico many years ago. [5] In fact, chili peppers have existed in North America for more than 8,000 years. [6] Have been a part of human civilization for a long time. [7] Today India is the largest producer, consumer and exporter of red chili peppers. [8] In fact, they account for 25 percent of India's spice export. [9] Chili peppers are very good for human health. [10] Just one-half cup (118 grams) of chopped chilies has 300 percent of the daily requirement for vitamin C. [11] Therefore, chili peppers benefit humans by making our food taste better and by improving our health.

Grammar Forms

11.1 Simple Sentences

A simple sentence contains one clause. A clause has a subject (who or what is doing the action) and a verb (what the action is).

1. 1 subject + 1 verb	Japan imports oil. 　　S　　　V
2. 1 subject + 2 or more verbs	Japan imports oil and exports vehicles. 　　S　　　V　　　　　　V
3. 2 or more subjects + 1 verb	Japan and China import oil. 　　S　　　　S　　　V Japan, China, and Cambodia import oil. 　　S　　　S　　　　　S　　　　V

Notes
1. A simple sentence has only one clause, which means one subject-verb combination. A simple sentence can have two subjects or two verbs, but there is only one subject-verb relationship.
2. Use a comma between three or more items in a series. Do not use a comma between two items.
    Japan, China, and Cambodia import oil.
    Japan and China import oil.
3. A sentence with two subject–verb relationships is called a compound sentence. (See Unit 12 for more on compound sentences.)
    Canada is the second largest country in the world, but it has only 39 million people.

11.2 Simple Sentence Word Order
Statements

1. subject + verb (+ object)	A destructive tsunami hit Japan in 2011.
2. prepositional phrase + subject + verb	In 2011, a destructive tsunami hit Japan.
3. subject + *be* + adjective	In many ways, German and English are similar.
4. subject + *be* + prepositional phrase	Germany is in Europe.

Commands

5. Verb (+ object + prepositional phrase) • The subject *you* is understood but not stated.	Let us consider the cost of importing oil. Please refer to my comments about your proposal.

11.2 Simple Sentence Word Order (continued)
Questions

6. helping verb + subject + verb • Helping verbs include *do, does, did, am, is, are, was, were, has, have, had, can, will.*	Did most immigrants come for economic reasons?
7. question word + helping verb + subject + verb	How do we know that the information is correct?
8. *be* + subject + adjective	Was the meeting necessary?
9. question word + *be* + subject	Who were the earliest explorers?

Notes
1. When a sentence begins with an introductory phrase, use a comma after the phrase.
   In many ways, German and English are similar.
2. In academic writing, 99 percent of sentences end in a period. Only about 1 percent of sentences are questions.

ACTIVITY 1

In each sentence, label each subject with *S* and underline each verb.

1. In 1990, West Germany and East Germany became one country again.

2. According to many scholars, Ernest Hemingway's works are definitely classics in American literature.

3. On July 23, 2012, Sally Ride became the first American woman to travel into space.

4. The ukulele and the mandolin are both string instruments.

5. Jackson Pollock and Willem de Kooning were artists of the abstract expressionism movement.

6. Writing a thank-you card does not take very much time and is not very difficult to do.

7. Unlike South Korea and Japan, Ecuador, Honduras, and the Philippines export bananas.

8. Nancy Love, Jacqueline Cochran, and Maggie Gee were female aviators and served during World War II.

Common Uses

11.3 Using Simple Sentences

The simple sentence is the most basic type of sentence. Use a simple sentence when there is a limited amount of information to explain. Use a simple sentence:

1. to state information • In academic writing, this is by far the most common use.	Barack Obama became president in 2009. This paper will discuss three aspects of the current economic situation in Argentina.
2. to give a command or make a request • This type of simple sentence is used in academic writing to direct the reader's actions.	Note the difference between these two types of animals. Let us now turn our attention to the third verb category.
3. to ask a question • In academic writing, this type of simple sentence is not used very often. It may be used in an essay introduction to grab the reader's attention (that is, as a hook) or in the concluding sentences.	How does aspirin work? This question has puzzled scientists for centuries. Perhaps the government's new plan is the best solution. Will it really solve the problem? Only time will tell.

ACTIVITY 2

In these sentences, label each subject with *S* and underline each verb. Then write *I* on the line if the sentence gives information, write *Q* if asks a question, or write *R* if it makes a request. Remember that a request does not have a subject.

_____ **1.** Of the world's 17 types of penguins, the largest penguins live in very cold climates.

_____ **2.** What factors impact the migration of manatees?

_____ **3.** Note the increase in oxygen flow in the next step of this experiment.

_____ **4.** For a variety of health reasons, the government should pass laws about smoking in public places.

_____ **5.** At this point, let us consider the differences between face-to-face and online classes.

_____ **6.** Without a doubt, physical exercise can greatly improve the health of young children.

_____ **7.** Imagine living in a world without the Internet.

_____ **8.** What roles will robots play in our future?

Common Errors

Common Error 11.1   Is there a complete verb form?

were

There ᴧ many problems in Nicaragua in the 1970s.

are

More and more parents ᴧ deciding to have smaller families.

REMEMBER: Every sentence must have a complete verb.

ACTIVITY 3   **Common Error 11.1**

Each sentence is missing a verb. Add a verb from the box below in the correct place in each sentence.

affects	check	enjoy	practice
causes	departed	launched	view

1. According to the news report, Senegal Airlines Flight 442 from Dakar at 11:15 a.m.

2. Motion sickness many people and consists of feeling nauseated in a moving car, bus, boat, or airplane.

3. Osteoporosis bones to become weak and fragile.

4. Pilatre de Rozier the first hot-air balloon in France in 1783.

5. The very best professional soccer players must for many years.

6. Many athletic people extreme sports such as skydiving, rock climbing, and snowboarding.

7. Before submitting essays, students should their writing for errors.

8. People can the aurora borealis in northern countries such as Canada and Iceland.

Common Error 11.2 Is there a subject?

It was
~~Was~~ perhaps the most important day in General Robert E. Lee's life.

REMEMBER: Every sentence needs a subject. In a command, the subject is *you*, but it is not written.

ACTIVITY 4 **Common Error 11.2**

Read the sentences. A missing subject is in parentheses. Use a caret (∧) to add the missing subject in the correct place. Use correct capitalization.

1. (*it*) The quarter is one of the most commonly used U.S. coins. Is worth 25 cents.

2. (*this purchase*) In 1867, the United States bought Alaska from Russia. At the time, was not very popular.

3. (*they*) For most beginners, Chinese writing symbols appear to be impossible to learn. However, with enough practice, are not so difficult.

4. (*they*) Hot springs have many healing powers. Can improve skin quality and reduce stress.

5. (*these two games*) Netball is a sport similar to basketball. Exactly how are similar?

6. (*people*) Frybread is a type of bread. Can eat it alone or with jam.

7. (*these beautiful animals*) Tigers are very big animals and can reach a body length of up to 11 feet (3.5 meters). Today live in China, Korea, and Russia.

8. (*It*) In 2009, a group of people discovered the largest cave in the world. Is located in Vietnam near the border with Laos.

Common Error 11.3 Do you have the correct punctuation for items in a series?

June, and

The months with the shortest names are May, ~~June and~~ July.

Africa and

Giraffes live in ~~Africa, and~~ eat leaves from the tops of trees.

REMEMBER: Use a comma to separate three or more items in a list. Do not use a comma for two items.

ACTIVITY 5 **Common Error 11.3**

In each sentence, add commas where they are needed. Some sentences do not need a comma.

1. The most popular tourist destinations in the United States are New York Chicago San Francisco Las Vegas and New Orleans.

2. Roses can grow in a variety of colors such as red yellow and white.

3. Two of the most popular picnic foods are fried chicken and potato salad.

4. June August September and October are the most common months to have a wedding.

5. Words such as swimming pool chocolate cake birthday gift and bus stop are examples of compound nouns.

6. Thailand shares a border with Myanmar Cambodia Laos and Malaysia.

7. More of the world's flags are white red and blue than any other color combination.

8. Many typical Louisiana dishes include green onions and celery.

Common Error 11.4 Is there a comma after an introductory phrase?

weather, Flight

Due to the bad ~~weather Flight~~ 833 departed late.

book, the

Near the end of the ~~book the~~ main character makes a huge mistake.

REMEMBER: Use a comma after any phrase that begins a sentence.

In each sentence, add commas where they are needed. Some sentences do not need a comma.

1. In October 1871 the weather in the Chicago area was extremely dry. From October 8th to October 10th a fire destroyed a large section of the city and killed 300 people.

2. Getting a college degree can certainly be expensive. For most people it is difficult to find a good job without one.

3. In both 2015 and 2016 the central part of the country received a record amount of rainfall.

4. At the end of the competition there was an award ceremony. The two players with the highest scores received awards.

5. Now let us consider the different qualities of each kind of rock. Between sedimentary and igneous rocks which of these is softer and therefore easier to damage?

6. To give their children the best education possible some parents teach their children at home. This practice is called home schooling and has become more and more popular recently.

There are about 2.3 million home-schooled students in the United States.

Academic Vocabulary

Words from the Academic Word List (Sublist 2)

affect	design	primary
categories	focus	region
complex	previous	strategies
consequences		

Source: Academic Word List (Coxhead 2000)

ACTIVITY 7   **Vocabulary in Academic Writing**

Use the academic vocabulary words to complete the sentences.

Subject Area	Example from Academic Writing
Political Science	1. The _____ reason for a national election is to choose the president of a nation.
Science	2. The creation of snow is a rather _____ process.
English Composition	3. What are the _____ of allowing a seven-year-old child to have a pet?
Education	4. Successful language learners report that using flashcards is one of the best _____ to learn a great deal of new vocabulary quickly.
Business	5. This paper will _____ on the early history of Apple computers.
Psychology	6. The school environment can _____ how children learn and communicate with their classmates.
Health	7. One _____ of the world with a very high life expectancy is Japan.
Chemistry	8. In the _____ experiment, we mixed sulfur and iron and saw an interesting result. However, in the next experiment, we will work with just sulfur.
Engineering	9. Many factors influence the _____ of a brand-new building.
Literature	10. Two _____ of literature include stories and poems.

Put It Together

Multiple Choice   Choose the letter of the correct answer.

1. A tiger is the national animal of Bangladesh, India _____ .

   a. and South Korea

   b. , and South Korea

   c. and, South Korea

   d. , South Korea

2. _____ showed the influence of Chinese literature.

   a. Because early works of Japanese literature

   b. With early works of Japanese literature

   c. Early works of Japanese literature

   d. Early works, of Japanese, literature

3. Three popular islands off the coast of Malaysia are _____ .

   a. Redang, Kapas, and Perentian

   b. Redang and Kapas and Perentian

   c. Redang, Kapas, Perentian

   d. Redang, and Kapas, and Perentian

4. The main difference among sedimentary, _____ the early development of each type.

   a. igneous, and metamorphic, rock

   b. igneous, metamorphic rock is

   c. igneous and metamorphic rock is

   d. igneous, and metamorphic rock is

5. In the Northern Hemisphere, _____ about 92 days long.

   a. spring and summer have

   b. spring and summer are

   c. spring, and summer have

   d. spring, and summer are

Error Correction   One of the five underlined words or phrases is not correct. Find the error and correct it. Be prepared to explain your answer.

6. Two similarities between <u>Ecuador and</u> <u>Indonesia, are</u> that both <u>countries are</u> on the <u>equator and</u> produce a large <u>amount of oil</u>.

7. <u>On</u> December 24, <u>1814, the</u> United <u>States and Great</u> Britain signed the Treaty of Ghent. After two years and eight <u>months, ended</u> the War of <u>1812 between the</u> two countries.

8. <u>Water</u> freezes <u>at 32 degrees</u> on <u>the</u> Fahrenheit <u>scale, and</u> <u>0 degrees</u> on the Celsius scale.

A violent tornado races across fields in Kansas.

ACTIVITY 9   **Building Greater Sentences**

Combine these short sentences into one sentence. You can add new words and move words around, but you should not add or omit any ideas. More than one answer is possible, but these sentences will be simple sentences.

1. a. Hurricanes can be terrifying.
   b. Hurricanes can be powerful.
   c. Hurricanes can be deadly.

   d. Tornadoes can be terrifying.
   e. Tornadoes can be powerful.
   f. Tornadoes can be deadly.

_____

_____

2. a. The Australian Open is a tournament.
   b. The French Open is a tournament.
   c. Wimbledon is a tournament.

   d. The U.S. Open is a tournament.
   e. The tournaments are for tennis.
   f. These are major tournaments.

_____

_____

3. a. The author Carlos Fuentes was born in 1928.
   b. The year of his death was 2012.

   c. He was Mexican.
   d. Carlos Fuentes was famous.

_____

_____

Steps to Composing

Read the paragraph. Then follow the directions in the 10 steps to edit the information and composition of this paragraph. Write your revised paragraph on a separate sheet of paper. Be careful with capitalization and punctuation. Check your answers with the class.

DESCRIPTIVE PARAGRAPH

Results of Commuting Survey

[1] For this assignment, we conducted a survey of students at Downtown University. [2] We wanted to know how many miles they commute each week. [3] We selected students at random from students entering the library. [4] We asked them one question. [5] The three answer choices were: under 20 miles (32 km) in a week, between 21 and 40 miles (34 and 64 km) in a week, and more than 40 miles in a week. [6] Out of 100 responses, 86 selected under 20 miles in a week. [7] We were surprised because we expected more people to report a higher weekly commuting distance. [8] The remaining answers were divided between the other two categories. [9] This information could be useful for future planning at Downtown University.

---

1. Use details in this academic report. In sentence 1, add the number of people in the study: 100.

2. In sentence 2, add the phrase *to the university* in an appropriate place to show where the students are commuting. In general, information about place goes before information about time.

3. To avoid repeating the same word, in sentence 3, change the first word *students* to *participants*.

4. This research took place on August 31, 2016. Add that date in the correct location in sentence 3.

5. In sentence 4, for a more precise meaning, change one to *a* and add the adjective *single*.

6. In sentence 4, add the prepositional phrase *about their commuting habits* to explain the question.

7. Sentence 7 has the pronoun *we* twice. Change *we were surprised* to *the results were surprising*.

8. In sentence 8, the percentage for the other two answers was, in fact, 7 percent. Because these groups had the same number, add the word *equally* or *evenly* after the verb *divided*.

9. In sentence 9, soften the conclusion by adding the words *we believe* in the correct place.

10. In sentence 9, add the word *transportation* to tell what kind of planning.

On a separate sheet of paper, write a descriptive paragraph (at least five sentences) with a topic sentence that lists three or four items. Introduce your list and then write about each of the items. If you wish, you may use the Internet to get facts, especially numbers, for your paragraph.

Here are some examples of how to begin.

- *In a study published in* . . . (name a journal), *researchers found that four excellent sources of vitamin C are* . . . .

- *In* (year), . . . *were the three highest paid athletes in* . . . (sport or country).

- *According to* . . . (the Canadian National Travel Office or similar), *the three most popular destinations in Canada are* . . . .

Young Japanese women enjoy a
roller coaster ride in Tokyo.

12 Using Compound Sentences

WHAT DO YOU KNOW?

DISCUSS Look at the photo and read the caption. Discuss the questions.

1. Are roller coasters popular in your country? Why or why not?
2. Do you enjoy riding a roller coaster? Why or why not?

FIND THE ERRORS This paragraph contains two errors with sentence structure. Find the errors and correct them. Explain your corrections to a partner.

DESCRIPTIVE PARAGRAPH

The Science Behind a Roller Coaster

[1] One of the most popular attractions at any amusement park is a roller coaster, very few people understand the science that explains how roller coasters work. [2] A roller coaster makes use of two different types of energy. [3] Potential energy is the energy that an object has because of its height. [4] Kinetic energy, on the other hand, is the energy that an object has because of its motion. [5] A roller coaster has multiple hills that it goes up during the trip. [6] The first hill is often a lift hill. [7] It has this name because there is a chain or other device that pulls the coaster up the first hill. [8] As the car goes higher, it builds greater potential energy. [9] This energy is released when the cars begin to go down the hill. [10] The actual movement of the cars is an example of the second type of energy, kinetic energy. [11] Most people do not know how a roller coaster works. [12] But they enjoy it just the same.

Grammar Forms

12.1 Compound Sentences

A compound sentence has two or more independent clauses that are connected by a coordinating conjunction. Three common coordinating conjunctions in academic writing are *and, but,* and *so.* They are also called *connectors.*

and	Mexico became independent in 1821, **and** Brazil became independent in 1822. S V S V
but	Japan imports oil, **but** Saudi Arabia exports it. S V S V
so	Malaysia lies near the equator, **so** its climate is very warm. S V S V

Notes
1. A compound sentence has two (or more) independent clauses, which means there are two (or more) subject–verb combinations.
2. A sentence with one subject–verb combination is called a simple sentence. (See Unit 11 for more information on simple sentences.)
3. Use a comma before the coordinating conjunction in a compound sentence.
4. Four other coordinating conjunctions that are used as connectors in compound sentences are *or, nor, for,* and *yet.* However, they are less common. Together these seven conjunctions are known as FANBOYS: *for, and, nor, but, or, yet, so.*

For each sentence, underline each subject and label each verb with *V*. Write *S* for a simple sentence and *C* for a compound sentence on the line.

_____ **1.** The tiny nation of Liechtenstein lies in central Europe and has no seacoast.

_____ **2.** At many universities, a major in history requires 36 credits of coursework, but a minor requires only 18 credits.

_____ **3.** In the words *string, French,* and *branch,* all of the letters but one are consonants.

_____ **4.** According to several Internet sources, the five most common surnames in England are Smith, Jones, Williams, Taylor, and Brown.

_____ **5.** Machu Picchu is a very popular destination, so Peru receives millions of tourists each year.

_____ **6.** The word *present* has two pronunciations, but the meanings are very different.

_____ **7.** Giraffes can eat up to 100 pounds of leaves per day, so they spend most of their day eating.

_____ **8.** Singapore has been an independent country for more than five decades, but it was part of Malaysia.

Singapore, with a population of 5.7 million people, is an island city-state located south of Malaysia.

Common Uses

12.2 Using Compound Sentences

Use a compound sentence when there is a logical connection between two ideas. The coordinating conjunction shows the relationship between the ideas.

1. Use *and* to add information	Brazil is in South America, **and** it has many beautiful beaches.
2. Use *but* to show a contrast	Canada is a very large country, **but** its population is small.
3. Use *so* to express a result	Australia was a British colony for a very long time, **so** the British influence there is strong.

Note
Do not use a comma with *so* when it introduces a purpose. With a purpose, *so (that)* means *in order that*.
  Scientists will conduct more experiments **so** (that) they can determine the effectiveness of a new medicine.

ACTIVITY 2

Fill in the blank with an independent clause to complete these compound sentences.

1. More people have cell phones now than at any other time in history, and _____

_____.

2. More people have cell phones now than at any other time in history, but _____

_____.

3. More people have cell phones now than at any other time in history, so _____

_____.

4. The first-class seats on most flights are very comfortable, and _____

_____.

5. The first-class seats on most flights are very comfortable, but _____

_____.

6. The first-class seats on most flights are very comfortable, so _____

_____.

Common Errors

Common Error 12.1 Is there a coordinating conjunction?

but
July is usually a month with a great deal of rainfall, this year it has been very dry.
                                                              ∧

REMEMBER: Use a coordinating conjunction in a compound sentence. A compound sentence that uses a comma without a conjunction is called a comma splice and is not correct.

ACTIVITY 3 **Common Error 12.1**

Read the following sentences. Add a comma in the correct place.

1. Brown rice and white rice are actually both rice but brown rice may be a healthier food choice.

2. Ten of the twelve South American countries have a coastline but Bolivia and Paraguay are landlocked.

3. The chemical symbol for silver is Ag and its atomic number is 47.

4. Most pencils in the United States have an eraser on top but most pencils in Europe have no eraser.

5. An apple typically has about 95 calories so it is a good choice for a healthy snack.

6. Bamboo is simply a kind of grass but more than 600 million people earn an income from bamboo.

7. Flying kites is a popular children's activity but it is a serious sport in several countries.

8. Three formats for vinyl records are 33, 45, and 78 but the 78 format record has always been the least common.

Common Error 12.2 Is a comma missing?

February has only 28 days, so it is the shortest of all the months.
                              ∧

REMEMBER: Use a comma before a coordinating conjunction when it connects two independent clauses.

In each sentence, one verb is missing. Use a verb from the box and correct the sentence. If needed, add a comma in the correct place.

affects	are	carry	follow
appears	arrived	find	guarantee

1. The very best professional soccer players must train for many years but their time on the field does not success.

2. According to the news report, Senegal Airlines Flight 442 departed from Dakar at 11:15 a.m. and it in Paris six hours later.

3. Before submitting essays, students should check their writing for errors so readers cannot easily errors in it.

4. Motion sickness is feeling nauseated in a moving car, bus, boat, or airplane but it people in very different ways.

5. People in northern countries such as Canada and Iceland can see the aurora borealis but it in the southern hemisphere at times.

6. Osteoporosis causes bones to become weak so people should their doctor's advice about this serious condition.

7. Many athletic people play extreme sports such as skydiving, rock climbing, and snowboarding so they obviously not afraid of injuries.

8. The first hot-air balloon flew in France but it did not people.

Common Error 12.3   Can you use a compound sentence?

, and koalas

Typical zoo animals represent many different continents. Giraffes live in Africa. ~~Koalas~~ are from Australia.

REMEMBER: Simple sentences are acceptable, but good writing uses a variety of both kinds of sentences. Avoid using too many short simple sentences.

ACTIVITY 5   **Common Error 12.3**

Read each set of sentences. Rewrite each pair into one sentence using *and, but,* or *so.* Be careful with punctuation.

1. Montana is the third largest U.S. state. It has a population of a little more than one million people.

_____

_____

2. Travelers can often find the same hotel room for different prices on different web sites. It is wise to look at several sites before booking.

_____

_____

3. Butterflies are beautiful creatures. Their average lifespan is only one month.

_____

_____

4. Carrots are rich in vitamin A. Carrots are easy to prepare.

_____

_____

5. Color psychology is the study of the effect of color on human behavior. Companies use research from color psychology to increase the sales of their products.

_____

_____

Common Error 12.4 Does the sentence begin with a coordinating conjunction?

dangerous, but
Spiders look ~~dangerous. But~~ not all spiders are poisonous.

REMEMBER: In academic writing, do not begin a sentence with *and*, *but*, or *so*.

ACTIVITY 6   **Common Error 12.4**

Read each sentence. If the sentence is good academic writing, write *Y* for *yes* on the line. Write *N* for *no* if it is not. If you write *N,* edit the sentence to improve it.

_____ 1. The first passenger elevator started service in New York. And this invention changed how cities could grow.

_____ 2. The weather in Texas is very hot during the summer months, so the best month for a vacation there might be October or November.

_____ 3. There is less demand for oil at the current time. So the price of oil has dropped a great deal.

_____ 4. The Academic Word List has 570 important words for university success. But a good student will need to know much more vocabulary than just these 570 words.

_____ 5. In Alaska, people can obtain a driver's license when they are 16½ years old. But in most states, a person has to be 18 for a driver's license.

_____ 6. For non-native speakers, one of the most difficult parts of English is the pronunciation of the letters *-ed* for past tense, so many students mispronounce *worked* as two syllables.

Academic Vocabulary

Words from the Academic Word List (Sublist 3)

document	instance	negative	removed	sufficient
initial	location	outcomes	sequence	task

Source: Academic Word List (Coxhead 2000)

ACTIVITY 7 Vocabulary in Academic Writing

Use the academic vocabulary to complete these sentences. For some, more than one answer is possible.

Subject Area	Example from Academic Writing
Physical Education	**1.** With first aid, the _____ response is very important, so quick action is necessary.
Science	**2.** The scientists did the same experiment with the same conditions four more times, but the _____ were different each time.
English Composition	**3.** A frequent _____ in many composition courses is to write an essay between 1,500 and 2,000 words, but many writers find this difficult.
Education	**4.** In order to earn a teaching license, a teacher must have _____ education as well as classroom experience.
Business	**5.** In this case, the company _____ part of its logo from its products, and sales increased a great deal.
Life Skills	**6.** A will is perhaps the most important _____ that any adult can possess, but many people have never written a will.
Health	**7.** Drinking sufficient water daily is important, but drinking too much water may have a _____ effect.
Mathematics	**8.** An even number can be divided by two evenly. For _____ , 10 and 26 are even numbers, but 11 and 27 are odd numbers.
Geography	**9.** The economy of a nation is connected to its _____ , but other factors are also important for an economy.
Literature	**10.** In any story, the motives of the characters and the _____ of events are important to understand the author's message.

Put It Together

ACTIVITY 8   Review Quiz

Multiple Choice   Choose the letter of the correct answer.

1. Brazil is a large country in South _____ the world's largest producer of coffee beans.

   a. America is   **b.** America and is   **c.** America and it is   **d.** America, is

2. Machu Picchu in Peru is one of the world's most popular tourist _____ the number of daily tourists is limited to 2,500 to protect the site.

   a. destinations, but   **c.** destinations but

   b. destinations,   **d.** destinations

3. A dozen items includes _____ dozen includes sixty.

   a. twelve, five   **b.** twelve five   **c.** twelve, so five   **d.** twelve so five

4. Baby rabbits are born _____ do not open their eyes until the 10th day after birth.

   a. hairless, so   **c.** hairless, they

   b. hairless, but   **d.** hairless, and they

5. Eating too much salt can be very bad for _____ urge people to consume less of it.

   a. people, so doctors   **c.** people, doctors

   b. people, but doctors   **d.** people doctors

Error Correction   One of the five underlined words or phrases is not correct. Find the error and correct it. Be prepared to explain your answer.

6. <u>The</u> 2022 FIFA World Cup championship <u>will take</u> place in <u>Qatar, so</u> the normal competition month of June or <u>July, it</u> has been changed <u>to</u> November.

7. According <u>to</u> a survey about <u>pet</u> ownership in <u>Canada, about</u> 35 percent of households <u>have</u> a <u>dog but</u> 38 percent have a cat.

8. Italy is <u>the</u> fourth largest economy in <u>Europe, and</u> its largest trading <u>partners, are</u> Germany, <u>France, the</u> United <u>States, and</u> Switzerland.

Jellyfish tentacles can be several feet long.

Building Greater Sentences

Combine these short sentences into one sentence. You can add new words and move words around, but you should not add or omit any ideas. More than one answer is possible, but they must be a compound sentence.

1. a. Most jellyfish live less than a year.

   b. The smallest live only a few days.

   c. Some of the smallest do this.

   d. The smallest are the size of a pinhead.

_____

_____

2. a. The most common allergy is to pollen.

   b. This allergy is for adults.

   c. Spring is a difficult time of the year.

   d. This time of the year is very difficult.

   e. This time of the year is difficult for those adults.

_____

_____

3. a. Celsius is a temperature scale.

   b. Celsius is a scale from the 1700s.

   c. Fahrenheit is a temperature scale.

   d. Fahrenheit is from the 1700s.

   e. More countries use Celsius now.

_____

_____

Read the paragraph. Then follow the directions in the 10 steps to edit the information and composition of the paragraph. Write your revised paragraph on a separate sheet of paper. Be careful with capitalization and punctuation. Check your answers with the class.

DESCRIPTIVE PARAGRAPH

The FIFA World Cup

[1] The FIFA World Cup is one of the most popular soccer events. [2] Many people would say it is the most important sports event in the world. [3] For example, the 2014 final game had an audience of 695 million. [4] The World Cup began in 1930. [5] It is less than 100 years old. [6] The World Cup is held every four years. [7] It is never held in the same year as the Olympics. [8] Eight different teams have won this event. [9] Brazil has won five times. [10] Germany has won four times. [11] Italy has won four times. [12] The other countries with one win are Uruguay, Argentina, England, France, and Spain.

---

1. In sentence 1, add the adverb *certainly* after the verb.

2. We need a transition word or phrase between sentences 1 and 2. Begin sentence 2 with *in fact*. Add a comma after an introductory phrase.

3. In sentence 3, add the phrase *between Germany and Argentina*.

4. In sentence 3, add the noun *viewers* in the correct place in order to be more specific.

5. Sentences 4 and 5 are short sentences. Combine them into a compound sentence with a good connector.

6. Sentences 6 and 7 discuss the same topic, so combine them into one compound sentence with a good connector.

7. In sentence 8, add the word *only* to emphasize the message of this sentence.

8. In sentence 8, add a powerful adjective such as *prestigious* to describe the World Cup.

9. Sentences 9, 10, and 11 are short sentences with similar information, so combine them into one compound sentence.

10. Read sentence 12 carefully. The information is correct, but in reality, Uruguay and Argentina have won twice. Add the phrase *at least* in the correct location, and this information will be clearer.

Original Writing

On a separate sheet of paper, write a descriptive paragraph (at least five sentences) that requires numbers such as years, population, or number of times (of an event). Make sure you include simple and compound sentences in your writing. Use at least two compound sentences. If you wish, you may use the Internet to get facts, especially numbers, for your paragraph.

Here are some examples of how to begin.

- *One of the most popular singers is . . . . Some of his/her most popular songs are . . . , . . . , and . . . .*

- *The top three world producers of . . . (name of product) are . . . , . . . , and . . . (names of countries).* (Give production data for each.)

- *The most common favorite colors are . . . , . . . , and . . . .* (Do Internet research on color psychology.)

An annual tomato-tasting event in Iowa draws huge crowds.

13 Writing with Adjectives

WHAT DO YOU KNOW?

DISCUSS Look at the photo and read the caption. Discuss the questions.

1. Why do you think people want to taste tomatoes? What does a tomato taste like to you?

2. What does a plant need to grow good tomatoes?

FIND THE ERRORS This paragraph contains two errors with adjectives. Find the errors and correct them. Explain your corrections to a partner.

NARRATIVE PARAGRAPH (SCIENCE REPORT)

The Effect of Sunlight on Plant Growth

[1] For my science project, I grew tomato plants in different light conditions to see how different amounts of light affect growth. [2] First, I selected 10 three-week-old plants that were similar in size. [3] I placed them in five locations very different. [4] Two plants received approximately one hour of full sunshine per day. [5] Two others received two hours of sunshine per day, two received three hours, two received four hours, and two received five hours. [6] All 10 plants were in the same type of soil and received the same amount of water each day. [7] After three weeks, the results showed that the plants that received more sunlight were an average of three inches taller than the plants that received less sunlight. [8] Though this experiment was quite simple, we can conclude that there is a relationship between the amount of sunshine and the amount of plant growth. [9] In other words, tomato plants in more bright locations generally experience more growth than those in conditions with less light.

Grammar Forms

13.1 Types of Adjectives

An adjective is a word that describes a noun or pronoun. There are different types of adjectives, but they all give information about a person, a place, or a thing. An adjective usually comes before a noun or after the verb *be*.

Types of Adjective	Adjectives	Examples in Sentences
Descriptive	*green, salty, delicious, sad*	Examples of **salty** foods include pretzels, French fries, and chips.
Possessive	*my, your, his, her, its, our, their*	Cats and rabbits are born with **their** eyes closed.
Demonstrative	*this, that, these, those*	**This** paper will answer three questions. **Those** plants grew very quickly.
Quantity	*some, two, fifty, many*	**Many** drivers have never had a car accident.
Nouns working as adjectives	*winter, car, chocolate, computer*	Snow and sleet are two examples of **winter** weather.
Comparative	*-er (newer), more (more recent)*	For customers who like **newer** computers, there is always a **more recent** version available.
Superlative	*-est (the newest), most (the most recent)*	**The newest** computer is expensive because it contains **the most recent** technology.

Notes
1. Three common endings for descriptive adjectives are *-y (cloudy, dirty)*, *-ful (careful, useful)*, and *-ous (dangerous, previous)*.
2. Comparative adjectives are often used with *than. The* comes before superlative adjectives.
   > This report is **more detailed than** the previous one.
   > The third report is **the most detailed** report of all.
3. Nouns that work as adjectives have different relationships. Here are some examples:
   > a **chocolate** cake: a cake made of chocolate
   > a **winter** coat: a coat used in the winter
   > a **passport** application: an application for the purpose of obtaining a passport
   > the **human** brain: the brain that is part of a human
4. Nouns used as adjectives are never plural, so we say *a **tomato** salad*, not *a tomatoes salad*.

13.2   Comparative Forms
Short adjectives

1. For one-syllable adjectives, add -*er*. If the adjective ends in -*e*, just add -*r*.	long—**longer** safe—**safer**
2. For two-syllable adjectives ending in a consonant + -*y*, drop the -*y* and add -*ier*	heavy—**heavier** wealthy—**wealthier**
3. When an adjective ends in a consonant-vowel-consonant, double the final consonant and add -*er*.	big—**bigger** wet—**wetter**

Long adjectives

4. For two-syllable adjectives that do not end in -*y*, use *more* + adjective.	famous—**more famous** polite—**more polite**
5. For adjectives with three or more syllables, use *more* + adjective.	important—**more important** comfortable—**more comfortable**

Irregular comparatives

6. Some adjectives have irregular comparative forms.	good—**better** bad—**worse**

13.3   Superlative Forms
Short adjectives

1. For one-syllable adjectives, add -*est*. If the adjective ends in -*e*, just add -*st*.	old—**the oldest** simple—**the simplest**
2. For two-syllable adjectives ending in a consonant + -*y*, drop the -*y* and add -*iest*.	easy—**the easiest**
3. When it ends in a consonant-vowel-consonant, double the final consonant and add -*est*.	thin—**the thinnest**

Long adjectives

4. For two-syllable adjectives that do not end in -*y*, use *most* + adjective.	famous—**the most famous** polite—**the most polite**
5. For adjectives with three or more syllables, use *most* + adjective.	important—**the most important** comfortable—**the most comfortable**

Irregular superlatives

6. Some adjectives have irregular superlative forms.	good—**the best** bad—**the worst**

For each underlined adjective in the sentence, write the type of adjective: descriptive, possessive, quantity, noun as adjective, or comparative.

1. The <u>main</u> reason for the <u>sudden</u> drop in <u>oil</u> prices is a severe lack of real demand.

_____

2. <u>Spaghetti</u> squash is a type of vegetable that is both <u>healthy</u> to eat and <u>simple</u> to prepare.

_____

3. College <u>science</u> textbooks have been increasing in price at a <u>tremendous</u> rate.

_____

4. In math, <u>negative</u> numbers always have a negative sign, but positive numbers can be written with or without the <u>positive</u> sign.

_____

5. In public speaking, believing what you are saying often has a much <u>larger</u> impact on <u>your</u> audience than simply saying the <u>right</u> words.

_____

6. College entrance exams traditionally feature <u>one</u> long <u>essay</u> question, but schools may now also require participation in a <u>group</u> discussion.

_____

7. There was an <u>old</u> science book and a bilingual dictionary on the <u>coffee</u> table.

_____

8. <u>His</u> favorite author, Anton Chekhov, was born in <u>southern</u> Russia on a <u>cold</u> day in January of 1860.

_____

Write the correct comparative or superlative form of the adjective in parentheses.

1. (*expensive*) Silver and gold are valuable, but gold is much

_____ than silver.

2. (*loud*) Most people do not know that elephants are perhaps the

_____ animals in a zoo.

3. (*healthy*) People who exercise on a regular basis and avoid eating fatty foods are

usually _____ than those who do not.

4. (*high*) Most of the _____ mountains in the world are

located in the Himalayas.

5. (*heavy*) In general, any air traveler with a suitcase that is

_____ than 50 pounds (23 kilos) has to pay an extra

baggage fee.

6. (*long*) How many letters does the _____ word in

English have?

7. (*dangerous*) Although many people are afraid of flying, driving a car is often

_____ than flying.

8. (*popular*) One of the _____ European countries for

tourists each year is Spain.

The Plaza de España in Sevilla, Spain was built in 1928 for the Ibero-American Exposition World's Fair.

Common Uses

13.4 Using Adjectives

Adjectives can do four things in a sentence. Adjectives can:

1. describe the noun they precede	Runners have to take extra care in **humid** weather.
2. describe a noun or pronoun being used as the subject of the sentence **a.** after the verb *be* **b.** after a linking verb (*appear, feel, look, seem, taste*)	The weather in Texas in summer is **hot**. The temperature seems **hotter** than it really is when there is no wind.
3. compare two or more nouns or pronouns	In the story, the main character is **lazier** than his sister Anna.
4. identify the item that is different in a group of three or more	The point in the ocean that is **farthest** from any land is in the South Pacific Ocean.

ACTIVITY 3

Fill in the blanks with an appropriate adjective from the box below.

cold	different	harder	large	similar
democratic	favorite	ideal	official	small

1. China and Brazil are very _____, but El Salvador and Belgium are very

_____ .

2. Costa Rica is a(n) _____ country in Central America.

3. January is not a(n) _____ month to visit Canada because the weather is so

_____ .

4. Spanish and Portuguese are _____ languages, but Chinese is very

_____ .

5. A treaty is a(n) _____ agreement between two or more countries.

6. For many high school students, algebra is _____ than geometry.

7. When people are asked what their _____ color is, the most common answers

are often blue, green, and red.

Common Errors

Common Error 13.1 Is the adjective in the correct position?

principal reason
Money is the ~~reason principal~~ for many arguments.

REMEMBER: An adjective usually comes before the noun it is describing. An adjective comes after *be* or a linking verb like *seem*.

ACTIVITY 4 **Common Error 13.1**

Draw a line through the adjective that is in the wrong place. Then write the adjective in the correct position using a caret (∧) and make any other necessary changes. Some sentences have more than one error.

1. Brown rice may be a food choice healthier than white rice.

2. Unfortunately, challenges budget will limit growth city in the next two to three years.

3. In my opinion, divorce is a problem social that we need to discuss more openly.

4. Regional food can tell us about the history of one area particular. For example, gumbo is a dish special from the state of Louisiana.

5. The cell phone is an invention modern.

6. Using a dictionary bilingual can be a method successful to learn new words.

7. There are differences significant between English British and English American.

8. There are many statistical methods for measuring satisfaction customer, but two are especially helpful for stores clothing.

Common Error 13.2 Is the adjective correct?

red
The liquids in the test tubes turned ~~reds~~.

REMEMBER: Adjectives are never plural. They have only one form.

ACTIVITY 5 **Common Error 13.2**

Write the plural of these sentences.

1. The other problem is also important.

2. This book is excellent.

_____

3. It is a huge environmental problem.

_____

4. An old car can be very expensive to maintain.

_____

5. A person likes to attend a cultural event.

_____

6. A female lion does 90% or more of the hunting.

_____

Common Error 13.3   Is the comparative form correct?

shorter
February is ~~more short~~ than the other eleven months.

REMEMBER: If an adjective has one syllable, add -_er_, or if it has two syllables and ends in -_y_, drop the _y_ and add -_ier_. For other adjectives, use the word _more_.

ACTIVITY 6   **Common Error 13.3**

Read each sentence. Underline the comparative form. If the comparative is correct, write _C_ on the line. If it is incorrect, write _X_ on the line. Cross out the error and write the correction above it.

_____ **1.** A few soccer players earn a more high salary than famous movie stars.

_____ **2.** Some people think it is more good to exercise in the morning than at night.

_____ **3.** Practicing something one hour every day is more helpful than practicing something for seven hours on only one day.

_____ **4.** For an English speaker, French is more easy to learn than Chinese.

_____ **5.** Good coaches encourage their players to have a more positive attitude.

_____ **6.** Most students would prefer to own a more light laptop.

_____ **7.** Japan has a more old written history than Canada.

_____ **8.** I have never met a more honest person than my mother.

Academic Vocabulary

Adjectives Frequently Used in Academic Writing

different	new	public
high	other	significant
important	political	social
international		

Source: Corpus of Contemporary American English (Davies 2008—)

ACTIVITY 7 Vocabulary in Academic Writing

Use the academic vocabulary to complete the sentences. For some sentences, more than one answer is possible.

Subject Area	Example from Academic Writing
Science	**1.** Some readers may think that bamboo and palm trees are similar, but they are in fact extremely _____ .
Business	**2.** Many times the success of a country's economy depends on the _____ party that is in power.
Life Skills	**3.** Knowing how to apply for a job is a(n) _____ skill to have.
Health	**4.** Many people do not like the idea of taking a(n) _____ medicine.
Physical Education	**5.** Playing a team sport is good exercise, but it is also a(n) _____ opportunity because you can meet many people.
Literature	**6.** In the story, Jackson climbs to the top of a very _____ mountain before he dies.
English Composition	**7.** Your instructor may give your paper a low grade if there are many _____ errors in it.
Education	**8.** Private schools can be excellent, but they cost much more than _____ schools.
Mathematics	**9.** The _____ solution to the problem resulted in the same final answer.
Geography	**10.** In some cases, _____ borders occur where there is a mountain range or a river.

Put It Together

Multiple Choice   Choose the letter of the correct answer.

1. Brazil is a _____ in South America.

   a. country large   **b.** large country   **c.** important country   **d.** country important

2. Cheddar and parmesan are varieties you can find in a _____.

   a. cheese store   **b.** store cheese   **c.** store of cheese   **d.** cheeses store

3. A _____ might be made of wool.

   a. winter's jacket   **b.** jacket of winter   **c.** winter jacket   **d.** jacket winter

4. Those are not _____ to this question.

   a. possible answer   **b.** possibles answers   **c.** possible answers   **d.** answers possibles

5. In order to succeed, this restaurant needs a more _____ interior design.

   a. strong   **b.** healthy   **c.** better   **d.** modern

Error Correction   One of the five underlined words or phrases is not correct. Find the error and correct it. Be prepared to explain your answer.

6. According to police <u>reports</u>, the fight between the <u>three men started</u> when one person became <u>angry</u> because the <u>line ticket</u> was moving <u>very</u> slowly.

7. When you <u>fill out the job application</u>, be <u>certain</u> to use <u>a blue or black pen</u> and <u>write</u> in <u>larges</u> letters.

8. As a <u>gift special</u> to say <u>thanks to someone</u>, roses seem to be <u>a</u> much <u>more popular</u> flower <u>than</u> orchids or tulips.

Seattle, Washington, is one of the fastest-growing cities in the United States.

ACTIVITY 9 **Building Greater Sentences**

Combine these short sentences into one sentence. You can add new words and move words around, but you should not add or omit any ideas. More than one answer is possible.

1. a. The rainfall is 38 inches.
   b. The rainfall is in Seattle.
   c. It is the average rainfall.
   d. It is the annual rainfall.

_____

_____

2. a. A shop is located near the bank.
   b. The shop sells flowers.
   c. The shop is excellent.
   d. The bank is new.
   e. The bank is by the river.

_____

_____

3. a. The experiment requires gloves.
   b. The gloves are cotton.
   c. The cotton is special.
   d. The experiment is about water.
   e. The water is from a lake.

_____

_____

Steps to Composing

Read the paragraph. Then follow the directions in the 10 steps to edit the information and composition of this paragraph. Write your revised paragraph on a separate sheet of paper. Be careful with capitalization and punctuation. Check your answers with the class.

COMPARISON PARAGRAPH

Alligators and Crocodiles

[1] People mistakenly believe that an alligator is the same as a crocodile. [2] In reality, these animals are extremely different. [3] One difference is location. [4] Alligators live in China and Florida. [5] Crocodiles live in Central America, northern South America, and northern Australia. [6] They are also in Southeast Asian countries such as Burma, Thailand, Malaysia, Singapore, and the Philippines. [7] Crocodiles are on almost every continent except Europe and Antarctica. [8] Also, crocodiles live in saltwater, but alligators do not. [9] A physical difference is the shape of their noses. [10] The nose of an alligator is sort of round. [11] A crocodile's nose is shaped like the letter V. [12] In addition, a crocodile's fourth tooth is visible when its mouth is closed. [13] An alligator's teeth are hardly visible when its mouth is closed. [14] Another general difference is that many types of crocodiles are more aggressive than most types of alligators. [15] In sum, they may look similar, but they are certainly different.

1. Sentence 1 is too strong. Not all people believe this incorrect information, so add the word *some*, *many*, or *most* in the correct place. Use the word that you believe is true.

2. In sentence 2, replace the word *animals* with the more accurate word, *reptiles*.

3. In sentence 2, add the adjective *two* in the best place.

4. Combine sentences 5 and 6.

5. Sentence 7 summarizes what is in sentences 5 and 6, so begin with the phrase *in other words*.

6. In sentence 7, change the noun *crocodiles* to a pronoun because the noun was used in the previous sentence, and it sounds repetitive.

7. In sentence 10, rewrite the subject to use a possessive form with an apostrophe.

8. Combine sentences 10 and 11 with the connector, *but*. Be careful with punctuation.

9. Begin sentence 13 with the phrase *in contrast*.

10. Sentence 15 has two pronouns, and one of them should be a noun. Change one of the pronouns to a noun. Possible answers include *alligators and crocodiles, these two reptiles, these two creatures,* and a few other possibilities.

| ACTIVITY 11 | **Original Writing** |

On a separate sheet of paper, write a comparison paragraph (at least five sentences) that compares two things. Use a good variety of adjectives.

Here are some examples of how to begin.

- *. . . and . . . may seem similar, but they are actually quite different.*
- *. . . and . . . may seem different, but in many ways they are similar.*
- *People often confuse . . . and . . ., but they are actually not so similar.*

The Pearl Monument, showing an oyster with a pearl inside, glows at night in Doha, Qatar.

14 Writing with Articles

WHAT DO YOU KNOW?

DISCUSS Look at the photo and read the caption. Discuss the questions.

1. Where do pearls come from?

2. Why are pearls popular?

FIND THE ERRORS This paragraph contains two errors with articles. Find the errors and correct them. Explain your corrections to a partner.

Pearls

¹ Like emeralds or diamonds, pearls are gemstones for the jewelry. ² However, unlike an emerald or a diamond, a pearl is not a stone found among rocks. ³ Instead, a pearl comes from a oyster, which is an animal that lives in a shell in the sea. ⁴ A pearl forms when a foreign particle gets inside the oyster and causes an irritation. ⁵ The oyster covers the particle with layers of a substance called nacre. ⁶ It is the nacre that gives a pearl its color and shine. ⁷ Pearls come in a variety of sizes, shapes, and colors. ⁸ The process of creating one pearl can take two to three years. ⁹ Before the 20th century, only wealthy people had pearls because natural pearls were very rare. ¹⁰ However, in the late 1900s, pearl farmers learned how to grow more pearls inside oysters. ¹¹ These pearls are called cultured pearls. ¹² Although both cultured and natural pearls are used in jewelry, cultured pearls are more popular.

Grammar Forms

14.1	Articles

Indefinite articles

a	Scientists are working on **a** cure for cancer.
	Use *a* before a singular noun that begins with a consonant sound, including the consonant sound /h/ (*hospital, house, happy*), or the letter "u" with the consonant sound /y/ (*university, unique*). **a** book, **a** good book, **a** university
an	Seafood is **an** excellent source of protein.
	Use *an* before a singular noun that begins with a vowel sound (*a, e, i, o*), the letter "u" with the vowel sound of ə (*umbrella, ugly*), or a silent "h" (*hour*). **an** example, **an** old book, **an** hour

Definite article

the	**The** islands of Indonesia have 40,000 varieties of plants.
	1. Use *the* before a singular noun. **the** book, **the** oldest book, **the** example **2.** Use *the* before plural count nouns. **the** books, **the** old books, **the** examples **3.** Use *the* before non-count nouns. **the** information, **the** recent information

No article (Ø)

1. Do not use an article with a non-count noun with a general meaning.

Salt can be a danger to **health**.

Climate scientists say more **research** should be done.

2. Do not use an article with a plural noun with a general meaning.

Dolphins make **noises** to communicate.

Notes
1. Quantity words can be used with plural nouns (*some examples, many books, a few diamonds*) and non-count nouns (*some water, more research, a lot of money, a little patience*).
2. Non-count nouns do not usually have a plural form (*research, health, information, patience, air, sand*).

Fill in the blank with the correct choice in parentheses. The symbol Ø indicates no article is needed.

1. The island of Sulawesi in Indonesia has _____ (a / an / Ø) unique ecosystem.

2. _____ (A / An / Ø) avalanche is a slide of snow on _____ (a / an / Ø) hillside.

3. Aquaculture is _____ (a / an / Ø) important part of Indonesia's economy.

4. When _____ (a / an / Ø) shark attack occurs near shore, it is usually during _____ (a / an / Ø) incoming tide.

5. According to _____ (a / an / Ø) recent research, walking for _____ (a / an / Ø) hour a day prevents weight gain.

6. _____ (A / An / Ø) hot topic is _____ (a / an / Ø) subject that everyone is talking about, while _____ (a / an / Ø) hot button issues cause anger.

7. Reading to children at _____ (a / an / Ø) early age will improve _____ (a / an / Ø) learning later in life.

8. The National Institutes of Health collects _____ (a / an / Ø) information on various diseases.

9. It is _____ (a / an / Ø) common knowledge that _____ (a / an / Ø) wealth is not necessary for happiness.

10. _____ (a / an / Ø) Tuberculosis (TB) is _____ (a / an / Ø) bacterial disease that spreads through the air when _____ (a / an / Ø) person with TB coughs or sneezes.

Common Uses

14.2 | Using *A, An*

Use *a* or *an* with a singular count noun when writing about one thing in general that is not specific or is the first reference.

> In 2001, **a** gemstone hunter in Brazil found **an** emerald that weighed 850 pounds (385 kilos).

14.3 | Using *The*

Use *the* when the noun is:

1. unique (when there is only one of something)	**The** heart receives signals from **the** brain.
2. specific (when it is part of a larger category, especially with expressions like *one of, some of, most of,* and with superlative adjectives)	**The** *janggu* is a type of drum played in traditional Korean music. One of **the** worst earthquakes this century happened in Haiti on January 12, 2010. Bahrain is **the** smallest country in the Middle East but it has one of **the** fastest growing economies.
3. the second mention	In 2001, a gemstone hunter in Brazil found an extremely large emerald. **The** emerald weighed 850 pounds (385 kilos).
4. shared knowledge (when the writer and reader are thinking about the same specific thing or person)	This section of **the** report includes a list of expenses. (*Both the writer and the reader know which report is being referred to.*)

Note
Use *the* with certain points of geography, including:
a. bodies of water (*the Amazon River*)
b. mountain ranges (*the Alps*), regions (*the Far East*)
c. place names that sound plural with words like *united, union, republic, kingdom, nation,* or
   the letter *-s* (*the United States, the Republic of Ireland, the Netherlands*)
   The exception is that no article is used with lakes (*Lake Michigan*).
   The Kingdom of Saudi Arabia is in **the** Middle East.

14.4 Using No Article (Ø)

Do not use an article:

1. with plural count nouns with a general meaning	**Ocean currents** can carry **seeds**.
2. with non-count nouns	**Wheat** and **rice** are very important crops.

ACTIVITY 2

Fill in the blank with the correct article: *a, an, the,* or *Ø* for none.

1. According to recent reports, approximately 50 percent of _____ fish we eat is from _____ fish farm.

2. Some historians think that _____ beginning of _____ Chinese civilization was 7,000 years ago.

3. For any new business, _____ financial investors will want _____ information on the possible risks.

4. Apple orchards do very well in _____ rich soil of _____ Columbia River region of _____ Oregon.

5. Samuel Adams was _____ American statesman and one of the signers of _____ Declaration of Independence in 1776.

6. _____ purpose of this report is to explain why ABM will be _____ most successful business model in selling _____ high-end merchandise.

7. Neil Armstrong was _____ first astronaut to step on _____ moon.

8. Many scientific reports show that _____ air pollution can cause _____ environmental problems.

Common Errors

Common Error 14.1 Do you use *a / an / the* in the correct places?

a
The Aral Sea in Central Asia is actually ∧ fresh water lake.

REMEMBER: Use *a / an / the* with singular count nouns. (Note: A singular count noun must have a word such as *a, an, the, this, that, my, your,* etc. in front of it. A singular count noun cannot be by itself.)

ACTIVITY 3 **Common Error 14.1**

Read each sentence. Then look at each underlined part. If the articles are correct, write *C* on the line in front of the sentence. If one or more articles are wrong, write *X* on the line. Then write the correction.

_____ **1.** On December 26, 2004, <u>earthquake</u> in the Indian Ocean created <u>giant tsunami waves</u> up to 100 feet (30.5 meters) high.

_____ **2.** Carbon dating can provide <u>an approximate date</u> for something that lived long ago.

_____ **3.** As part <u>of advertising campaign</u>, some companies create <u>a slogan</u>, which is <u>a phrase</u> like Nike's "Just Do It."

_____ **4.** The Volga River in Europe was <u>an important trade route</u> for the early Vikings and Central Asians.

_____ **5.** An Ironman Triathlon consists of a 2.4-mile (3.7 km) swim, <u>an 112-mile (180 km) bike ride</u>, and <u>a 26.2-mile (42 km) run</u>.

_____ **6.** "The Gift of the Magi" is <u>a story</u> about a married couple without <u>a money</u> for gifts.

_____ **7.** Rather than giving birth to <u>a baby</u> in <u>an hospital</u>, some women choose to give birth at <u>home</u>.

_____ **8.** In some places, driving <u>a car</u> while texting is <u>a crime</u> that can result in <u>an expensive</u> ticket.

Common Error 14.2 Do you use *a / an* with a non-count noun?

The students will conduct a research on laboratory mice this semester.

REMEMBER: Do not use *a / an* with non-count nouns.

In each sentence, find the error and mark the correction. There may be more than one error.

1. Most people use an ATM machine to withdraw a money from a bank.

2. The latest research shows an evidence that beetles pollinated plants millions of years ago.

3. The data revealed a great deal of an information about droughts in the past.

4. In 2016, there was a 2.3 percent drop in sales of a jewelry in the United States.

5. The website provides an advice on how to set up your own small business web page, including a free software.

6. To be effective, a homework should reinforce what students have learned in class.

7. For more than 15 years, crews on the International Space Station have provided a view on a life in a space.

8. A people from the local community have helped to plan a new park that will open in the spring of next year.

Common Error 14.3 Do you need *the*?

Researchers are trying to understand how ~~the~~ tornadoes stop.

Many health problems are because of ~~the~~ pollution.

REMEMBER: Do not use *the* before nouns when you mean the category in general (*all tornadoes; all pollution*).

ACTIVITY 5   Common Error 14.3

Read the following sentences. Underline the nouns. If all the articles are correct, write *C* on the line in front of the sentence. If one or more articles are wrong, write *X* on the line. Then write the correct article(s) above the sentence.

_____ 1. Indonesia's forests are being cut down to make room for the agriculture.

_____ 2. Some people believe that the music can help plants grow.

_____ 3. One of the finest examples of French baroque architecture is the Palace of Versailles.

_____ 4. The theme of the song "Rolling in the Deep" by Adele is the heartbreak.

_____ 5. The architectural style of Frank Lloyd Wright included clean lines and open rooms.

_____ 6. One problem with the technology is that some users fail to read the instructions.

_____ **7.** Because the overcrowding at an international football match can be a safety hazard, organizers should plan for any potential problems.

_____ **8.** Recent research found that adopted children may remember the sounds of the language they heard as babies.

ACTIVITY 6 **Common Errors 14.1, 14.2, and 14.3**

In each set of sentences, fill in the blank with the correct article (*a, an, the,* or Ø for none).

1. This report will discuss _____ new type of phone technology that has many

   advantages over _____ current system. Additionally, we present _____

   new policy that will guarantee full support of _____ new technology by the sales team.

2. Some people buy their food from _____ local farmers because of _____

   personal health concerns, but these purchases are also promoting _____ economic

   health of _____ local community.

3. Fibonacci numbers are 0, 1, 1, 2, 3, 5, 8, 13, 21, and so on, where _____ next number

   is the sum of _____ two numbers before it. Mathematicians can see Fibonacci

   numbers in patterns that occur in _____ nature. For instance, this number pattern

   appears in the spirals of _____ pineapple, the petals of a flower, and the flowers on

   _____ artichoke plant.

The spirals of artichoke flowers reflect a mathematical pattern.

Academic Vocabulary

Nouns Frequently Used with *An* in Academic Writing

attempt	element	explanation	instrument	opportunity
effort	examination	increase	object	overview

Source: Corpus of Contemporary American English (Davies 2008–)

ACTIVITY 7 **Vocabulary in Academic Writing**

Use the article *an* and the academic vocabulary to complete the sentences. For some sentences, more than one answer is possible.

Subject Area	Example from Academic Writing
Nursing	**1.** A nurse anesthetist must give _____ of the surgery process to the patient.
Health	**2.** Research shows that learning to play _____, such as a piano or flute, can lessen the aging of the brain.
Criminal Justice	**3.** A criminology study looked at the effect of shorter jail time as _____ to reduce crime.
Economics	**4.** The theory of capitalism says that everyone has _____ to work hard and become wealthy.
Civil Engineering	**5.** An aerial view of Mesopotamia will show _____ in the number of canals restored for crop irrigation, fish farms, and flood control.
Industrial Engineering	**6.** This report will provide _____ of the current manufacturing systems and the types of injuries that employees report.
Physics	**7.** If a rocket traveling at 26,000 mph (41,843 kph) hit _____ in space, the collision would create a lot of space debris.
Ecology	**8.** Due to the increasing demand for water, it is important that utility companies make _____ to repair leaky pipes.
Public Health	**9.** To prevent a global epidemic, some countries require travelers who are leaving an area infected by the Ebola virus to have _____ by a doctor.
Art History	**10.** In his paintings of water lilies, Monet used cool watercolors as _____ of design.

Put It Together

Multiple Choice   Choose the letter of the correct answer.

1. The island of Yakushima, Japan, has _____ ancient forest that has never been cut.

   a. Ø   **b.** a   **c.** an   **d.** the

2. Copper is a valuable metal that can conduct _____ heat and electricity.

   a. Ø   **b.** a   **c.** an   **d.** the

3. The true story of Carl Brashear, as it is told through the movie *Men of Honor*, is _____ inspiration to anyone with a dream to do something despite the odds.

   a. Ø   **b.** a   **c.** an   **d.** the

4. In literature, a fairy tale usually includes a villain, a victim, and _____ hero.

   a. Ø   **b.** a   **c.** an   **d.** the

5. Ravi Shankar was an Indian musician who received awards from around _____ world.

   a. Ø   **b.** a   **c.** an   **d.** the

Error Correction   One of the five underlined words or phrases is not correct. Find the error and correct it. Be prepared to explain your answer.

6. Sacajawea was a Native American woman who belonged to the Shoshone tribe. She played a important role in the success of the Lewis and Clark expedition across the American interior in 1804. She acted as an interpreter and guide.

7. A group of farmers held a brainstorming session to develop ideas for reducing soil erosion in the Palouse River Basin. One of an ideas was to change the way that the farmers were putting seeds into the ground.

8. Meteorologists use satellite images to predict a weather and advise the public. A satellite image shows clouds and their movements, and an infrared image shows temperatures.

Komodo dragons live on islands in Indonesia.

ACTIVITY 9   **Building Greater Sentences**

Combine these short sentences into one sentence. You can add new words and move words around, but you should not add or omit any ideas. More than one answer is possible, but these sentences require the correct use of articles.

1. **a.** Komodo dragons are giant lizards.
   b. They can grow to be 10 feet (3 meters) long.
   c. They can weigh 300 pounds (136 kilos).
   d. They are from Indonesia.

   _____

   _____

2. **a.** A hurricane is a large storm.
   b. It has winds of 75 to 200 miles (121 to 322 kilometers) per hour.
   c. The wind speeds are continuous.

   _____

   _____

3. **a.** A tsunami is an ocean wave.
   b. It is a large wave.
   c. It is caused by an earthquake.
   d. The earthquake is on the ocean floor.

   _____

   _____

Steps to Composing

Read the paragraph. Then follow the directions in the 10 steps to edit the information and composition of this paragraph. Write your revised paragraph on a separate sheet of paper. Be careful with capitalization and punctuation. Check your answers with the class.

DEFINITION PARAGRAPH

Farming for Fish

[1] Fish farming is a type of commerce that grows fish as food for humans. [2] Instead of catching fish from boats, fish farmers can raise fish in ponds that are man-made. [3] The farmer can also raise fish in cages that are in the sea or in tanks that are inside buildings. [4] The type of fish plays a role in the size of the pond, cage, or tank. [5] The type also determines the kind of food. [6] The method of farming determines the number of ponds. [7] The farmers can buy baby fish from a supplier, or they can raise their own. [8] When the babies are large enough, the farmer moves them to a larger pond. [9] After several months, the fish will be ready to harvest and sell. [10] Fish farming can be a very good business because of the demand. [11] Fish is a good source of protein. [12] The oceans are overfished. [13] The human population is growing. [14] Fish farming is a good alternative to ocean fishing.

---

1. In sentence 2, write *boats* as singular. Remember the article.

2. In sentence 2, change *farmers* and *ponds* to singular. Make the verbs agree with these singular nouns. Remember the articles.

3. In sentence 3, change *cages*, *tanks* and *buildings* to singular. Make sure the verbs agree with these singular nouns. Remember the articles.

4. Combine sentences 2 and 3 to list the three ways of farming in one sentence. Start by removing *The farmer can also raise* from sentence 3. Put a comma after *man-made* in sentence 2 in place of the period. Then put a comma after *sea*.

5. Sentence 5 needs an example. Add a new sentence after sentence 5: *For example, tilapia can eat a plant-based food, but salmon need a fish-based food.*

6. The verb in sentences 5 and 6 is the same. In sentence 6, change *determines* to *establishes* for better variety.

7. Sentence 7 needs information about how the farmer raises the babies. At the end of sentence 7, add *in a separate, smaller pond*.

8. Add a detail about the size of the baby fish in sentence 8. After the word *enough*, add a comma and the phrase *usually 5 cm* followed by another comma.

9. Combine sentences 11, 12, and 13. At the end of sentence 11, replace the period with *but* plus a comma. At the end of sentence 12, replace the period with *and* plus a comma.

10. Connect sentence 14 to the previous information by adding *For these reasons,* to the beginning of it.

ACTIVITY 11   Original Writing

On a separate sheet of paper, write a definition paragraph (at least five sentences) about a particular person, animal, or thing. Use examples of the articles *a, an,* and *the*. When you have finished, underline all of the articles you used.

Here are some examples of how to begin:

- *A judge is an official who must make decisions in cases where people disagree on what to do.*
- *A dragonfly is an insect with a double set of long wings.*
- *An industrial engineer is a professional who works to make systems operate efficiently.*

Basketball superstar Kevin Durant volunteers as a coach at a special youth basketball event.

15 Writing with Adverbs

WHAT DO YOU KNOW?

DISCUSS Look at the photo and read the caption. Discuss the questions.

1. Why do you think Durant volunteers to coach children?

2. What are some of the characteristics of a professional athlete?

FIND THE ERRORS This paragraph contains two errors with adverbs. Find the errors and correct them. Explain your corrections to a partner.

OPINION PARAGRAPH

Kevin Durant: A True Sportsman

[1] Despite the fact that Kevin Durant is one of the highest-paid athletes in the National Basketball Association (NBA), nearly everyone who is involved with professional basketball says that he is very kind and down-to-earth. [2] In fact, an athletic footwear company once made several commercials calling Durant "the nicest guy in the NBA." [3] Even before Durant began playing basketball professionally in 2007, his goal was to help young boys by coaching them in basketball. [4] Today he generously gives millions of dollars to charities, and he reminds often boys that they can be both strong and kind. [5] Perhaps Durant learned this attitude from his first coach, who guided him personal through high school. [6] Obviously, this coach meant a lot to him. [7] Today Durant respectfully wears the number 35 on his jersey because 35 was the coach's age when he tragically died. [8] It is clear that Kevin Durant is a true sportsman because he is athletic, kind, and generous.

Grammar Forms

There are different types of adverbs: adverbs of place, time, frequency, manner, certainty, and degree. Adverbs give information about a verb, adjective, or adverb.

Adverbs have many positions in sentences, including before or after a verb, after an object, and before an adjective.

Subject	Auxiliary	Adverb	Verb	Object	Adverb	Adjective
The sun	can	**easily** (*manner*)	burn	a person.		
Lightning	can		occur		**everywhere**. (*place*)	
Lightning			is		**clearly** (*certainty*)	dangerous.
Lions		**usually** (*frequency*)	hunt	smaller animals	**at night**. (*time*)	
Alligators			are		**extremely** (*degree*)	strong.

Notes
1. Adverbs can be formed by adding -*ly* to the end of an adjective: *quick* → *quickly*. For adjectives ending in *y*, change *y* to *i* and add -*ly*: *easy* → *easily*.
2. Many adverbs do not end in -*ly*: *fast, hard, well, seldom, often, very, so, too, quite, maybe.*
3. The adverbs *fast* and *hard* can also be adjectives describing nouns.
   Everyone wants **fast** Internet speed.
4. Not all words that end in -*ly* are adverbs. These words are adjectives: *friendly, lonely, lovely, costly, timely, scholarly.*
5. Prepositional phrases can also function as adverbs by telling where (*in France*), when (*at noon*), how (*by car*).

For each adjective in parentheses, write the correct adverb on the line. Then underline the verb that it modifies.

1. The government should act _____ (*quick*) to provide money for flood victims.

2. If a player _____ (*complete*) misses the hoop, he or she loses a turn as well as two points.

3. All of the team members worked _____ (*hard*) to launch the new web site.

4. Engineers look at how processes can work more _____ (*efficient*).

5. According to the nuclear plant inspectors, all the systems are operating _____ (*safe*).

6. The World Meteorological Organization assigns names to tropical storms _____ (*alphabetical*).

7. A person with insomnia cannot sleep _____ (*good*).

8. You can _____ (*easy*) distinguish a 747 from other airplanes because of its unique shape.

Common Uses

15.2 Adverbs of Place and Time

Adverbs can describe *where* and *when* the action of the verb happens.

Place: *here, there, far, somewhere, in, on, at*

Time: *first, then, next, last, before, after, recently, soon, later, early, finally*

Position	Example
1. Adverbs of place come *before* adverbs of time.	President Lincoln was shot **inside Ford's Theater in 1865**. place time
2. Adverbs of time are sometimes at the beginning for emphasis or for cohesion. (Cohesion refers to how sentences are logically connected.)	**Soon after** the earthquake, a giant tsunami hit the shore of Fukushima. **First**, a 9.0 earthquake occurred under the ocean floor. **Then** it created a giant tsunami that hit Fukushima 50 minutes **later**.

15.3 Adverbs of Frequency

Adverbs of frequency describe *how often* an action happens.

0%   50%   100%

never   rarely   seldom   sometimes   often   usually   always

⟷

Position	Example
1. before the verb	Hurricanes **often** cause flooding.
2. after *be*	Male baldness is **usually** hereditary.
3. between the auxiliary and main verb	We may **never** find intelligent life in another galaxy.

Notes

1. The adverbs *usually*, *generally*, and *sometimes* can go at the beginning of a sentence.
2. The frequency adverbs *never*, *rarely*, and *seldom* have a negative meaning. Do not use another negative word (*no, not, none, no one, nothing*) in the same sentence.
3. Adverbs that tell the specific frequency are usually at the end of a sentence.
   In this experiment, the biologist checked the water temperature **daily**.

15.4 Adverbs of Manner

Adverbs of manner describe *how* something happens: *well, fast, hard, easily, badly, exactly, closely, loudly, perfectly, precisely, repeatedly, safely, quickly, slowly, recently, carefully.*

Position	Example
1. after the object of a verb	Members of Congress should read the <u>reports</u> **carefully**. *O*
2. after a verb (when there is no object)	The experiment <u>went</u> **well**. *V*
3. between the auxiliary and verb	During a typhoon, a river <u>can</u> **quickly** <u>overflow</u> its banks. *aux* *V*

Notes
1. Never put the adverb between the verb and object.
   The doctor read ~~quickly~~ the lab results.
2. Adverbs of manner come after the verb, but can come before for particular emphasis.
   She **quickly** read the document.

15.5 Adverbs of Certainty

Adverbs of certainty express probability, or describe how certain we are that something exists or happens: *definitely, certainly, clearly, possibly, likely, probably, perhaps.*

Position	Example
1. before a verb	The Inca Indians **likely** <u>died</u> from a disease.
2. after the verb *be*	The long-term effects of eating salty food <u>are</u> **clearly** harmful.

Note
1. *Maybe* and *perhaps* often go at the beginning of a sentence. In academic writing, *perhaps* is much more common than *maybe*.

15.6 Adverbs of Degree

Adverbs of degree describe to what degree or extent something happens: *hardly, barely, almost, only, just, nearly, mainly, completely, extremely, quite, enough, very, so, too.*

Position	Example
1. before adjectives or adverbs	Running a 10-kilometer race can be **extremely** difficult. The bullet trains in Japan travel **very** fast.
2. before the verb, or between auxiliary and base verb	Some viruses can **completely** destroy a computer.
3. *so, too, very* (intensifiers) go before an adjective or adverb	Driving **too** slowly on interstate highways can be dangerous.
4. *enough* goes after a verb or adjective	The planet Venus is hot **enough** to melt lead.

Notes
1. Do not confuse *very* and *too*. *Very* is used for emphasis. *Too* means excessively and suggests that something is impossible.
   The hill is **very** steep. = It will be difficult to climb.
   The hill is **too** steep. = It is impossible to climb.
2. The adverbs *barely, hardly,* and *rarely* have a negative meaning. Do not use another negative word in the same sentence.

ACTIVITY 2

Underline the adverb(s) in each sentence and the verb or adjective that it modifies. Then write the adverb type (*time, frequency, manner, certainty,* or *degree*) on the line. Some sentences may have more than one adverb.

1. Residents of the United States must file an income tax report annually. _____

2. It is nearly impossible to drive an electric car fast. _____

3. Coal miners in that area work very hard. _____

4. The gray timber wolf often travels in a pack with other wolves. _____

5. Cultural differences are usually the cause of misunderstandings. _____

6. North American bats mainly sleep in trees during the day. _____

7. The Egyptian queen Cleopatra likely died from a snake bite. _____

8. Some fruit trees will only produce fruit every two years. _____

Write a sentence by putting the words and phrases in the correct order. In some cases, there is more than one correct answer.

1.

| animal on our | 18 feet tall | sometimes | and weigh about 3,000 pounds |
| grow nearly | planet and can | a giraffe | is the tallest |

2.

| sometimes frighten | lightning may | only | kill people |
| lightning can | actually | thunder and | people, but |

3.

| animals are the same | have never | between an alligator | learned the difference |
| believe these two | and a crocodile, | many people | and some erroneously |

4.

| requires | a relatively | easily | a food that | many inexperienced cooks |
| because it | salmon is | quite | can burn | short cooking time |

5.

| people include | at least | the word ICE stands for | IN CASE of EMERGENCY, and |
| phone directory | in their | one ICE entry | it is strongly recommended that |

Common Errors

Common Error 15.1   Do you use the adverb form of the word?

> *softly*
> The orchestra played ~~soft~~ while the soloist performed.

REMEMBER: Put the *-ly* ending on an adjective to describe the manner that (how) something is done.

Common Error 15.2   Is the adverb of manner in the correct position?

> *carefully*
> The biologist held ~~carefully~~ the owl.
>   ∧

REMEMBER: Never put an adverb between a verb and object.

ACTIVITY 4   Common Error 15.1 and 15.2

Underline the adverb in the parentheses that correctly completes each sentence.

1. The heat shield on the space shuttle *Discovery* was (*badly damaged / damaged bad*) during the rocket lift off in 2005. Once the shuttle (*safely was / was safely*) in orbit, astronauts performed a spacewalk and repaired (*the shuttle successfully / successfully the shuttle*).

2. At a young age, Victor Borge played (*classical piano excellently / excellently classical piano*). He also had a very (*well / good*) sense of humor. For his concerts, he dressed (*formal / formally*) and sat (*properly / proper*) at the piano. He always played (*beautiful / beautifully*). However, in the middle of a song, he sometimes stopped (*unexpected, unexpectedly*) and did something that caused the audience to laugh loudly. Victor Borge performed (*this act repeatedly / repeatedly this act*) for years. He holds the world's record for the longest running one-man show on Broadway.

Common Error 15.3 Is the frequency adverb in the correct position?

often
During the 1600s, sailors died ~~often~~ from lack of vitamin C.

three times
The researchers ~~three times~~ repeated the experiment.

REMEMBER: • Adverbs of frequency go before the verb but after *be*.
• Adverbs of specific frequency usually go at the end of the sentence.

ACTIVITY 5 Common Error 15.3

Read the following sentences. Underline the adverb of frequency in each sentence. If the adverb form and position is correct, write *C* on the line. If the adverb form or position is wrong, write *X* on the line. Then write the correction above the sentence.

_____ **1.** We add an extra day every four years to the calendar.

_____ **2.** Some people believe that lightning never strikes in the same place twice.

_____ **3.** People who try to predict the direction of tornadoes are wrong often.

_____ **4.** Always tsunamis begin with the water flowing away from shore.

_____ **5.** Penguins often swim in freezing water, but their feathers collect rarely ice.

_____ **6.** Wind damage usually is a problem with hurricanes.

_____ **7.** Snow avalanches are almost never a result of loud noises.

_____ **8.** When an avalanche buries someone in snow, that person seldom survives.

Common Error 15.4   Is the adverb of degree correct and in the correct position?

very
The economy of Germany is ~~too~~ strong now.

a
The company barely made ~~no~~ profit last year.

big enough
Some snakes are ~~enough big~~ to swallow a pet.

REMEMBER: • *Too* means it is excessive and a problem.
   • Do not use double negatives.
   • Put *enough* after an adjective.

ACTIVITY 6   **Common Error 15.4**

Underline the adverb in each set of parentheses that correctly completes each sentence. There are adverbs of degree and other types of adverbs in this activity.

1. Many children spend (*too much / enough*) time playing video games and (*not enough / not barely*) time studying.

2. Professional basketball player Kevin Durant is (*very tall / too tall*) and has long arms. Opponents (*can, cannot*) rarely stop his plays.

3. Scientists (*recently discovered / discovered recently*) a coral reef near the mouth of the Amazon River. The water there is (*so muddy / very muddy*) that (*hardly no one / hardly anyone*) can see the reef.

4. When the scientists looked at the results of the experiment, they realized the study was (*wrong completely / completely wrong*). They did not have (*a large enough sample / a large sample enough*).

5. The godwit birds of Alaska can fly (*too fast / very fast*) and reach New Zealand in nine days. In order to do this, they (*rarely / do not rarely*) sleep or eat.

6. In police work, DNA evidence (*can help certainly / can certainly help*) in finding a criminal, but it is very important that they have (*enough / too many*) DNA samples.

7. Geologists know that it (*nearly is impossible / is nearly impossible*) to predict an earthquake.

8. A hippopotamus is (*so / too*) strong that it can kill an alligator.

Academic Vocabulary

Adverbs Frequently Used with *Very* in Academic Writing

carefully	likely	recently
clearly	often	slowly
closely	quickly	well
far		

Source: Corpus of Contemporary American English (Davies 2008–)

ACTIVITY 7   Vocabulary in Academic Writing

Use the academic vocabulary to complete the sentences. For some sentences, more than one answer is possible.

Subject Area	Example from Academic Writing
Sociology	**1.** Until very _____, women in Saudi Arabia did not vote.
Archaeology	**2.** Archaeologists are looking at evidence that suggests that the Vikings very _____ explored North America 500 years before Columbus.
Chemistry	**3.** Before repairing a valuable painting, chemists must very _____ examine the chemicals used in the paint hundreds of years ago.
Health Sciences	**4.** For some people with back and neck pain, acupuncture works very _____ .
Law	**5.** The United Nations Declaration of Human Rights very _____ states that everyone has the right to an education, but millions of children never attend school.
Nursing	**6.** People with diabetes must check their blood sugar levels very _____ .
Industrial Engineering	**7.** As part of the review, our team recommends purchasing a shuttle bus to take hotel guests to the convention center because the parking lots can very _____ fill with cars
Medical Technology	**8.** Doctors are not very _____ from being able to do brain surgery with ultrasound instead of a knife.
Public Relations	**9.** When television networks conduct public opinion surveys of politicians, the results are very _____ negative.
Geology	**10.** Water flows through sand quickly, but it moves very _____ through rock and clay.

Put It Together

Multiple Choice Choose the letter of the correct answer.

1. Space suits must be _____ to withstand hits from micrometeorites.

   a. enough strong   **b.** strong enough   **c.** too strong   **d.** strongly

2. Environmental engineers are working on technology that will _____ from water.

   a. remove economical salt   **c.** remove economically salt

   b. economical salt remove   **d.** remove salt economically

3. Mother Teresa of Calcutta was _____ .

   a. a kindly very woman   **c.** a woman very kindly

   b. a very kind woman   **d.** a woman very kind

4. According to veterinarians, horses _____ birth to triplets.

   a. give rarely   **b.** give rare   **c.** rarely give   **d.** rare give

5. After the 2010 earthquake, humanitarian groups sent _____.

   a. to Haiti supplies immediately   **c.** immediately to Haiti supplies

   b. immediately supplies to Haiti   **d.** supplies to Haiti immediately

Error Correction One of the five underlined words or phrases is not correct. Find the error and correct it. Be prepared to explain your answer.

6. In the near future, better telescopes will allow scientists to observe some very remarkably processes

   in space. For example, they will likely see the earliest stages of galaxy formation.

7. In the Gulf of Mexico, fishermen sometimes catch mantis shrimp that are up to 15 inches long. These

   shrimp are very territorial and fight often other mantis shrimp. They live in the rocks and rarely come out.

8. People see occasionally lightning without hearing thunder, and sometimes they hear thunder without

   seeing lightning. However, thunder and lightning always occur together. If the sound is not heard, it is

   because the lightning is too far away. If the lightning is not seen, it is hiding inside a cloud.

A baby elephant crosses a river with an elephant herd in Kenya.

ACTIVITY 9   **Building Greater Sentences**

Combine these short sentences into one sentence. You can add new words and move words around, but you should not add or omit any ideas. More than one answer is possible, but these sentences require adverbs.

1. a. This action was last year.
   b. The elephant could not do something.
   c. The elephant was a baby.
   d. The action was not easy.
   e. The action was to cross the river.

_____

_____

2. a. A groom serenades a bride with music.
   b. This usually happens.
   c. This is outside her house.
   d. This is the night before a Colombian wedding.

_____

_____

3. a. Emergency personnel worked.
   b. Their action was quick.
   c. It was to find earthquake survivors.

_____

_____

Read the paragraph. Then follow the directions in the 10 steps below to edit the information and composition of this paragraph. Write your revised paragraph on a separate sheet of paper. Be careful with capitalization and punctuation. Check your answers with the class.

PROCESS PARAGRAPH

Collecting Water from Air

[1] If you cannot find water, you can use basic science knowledge to create a water collector with a few simple steps. [2] First, find a container, such as a bowl or a pan, a sheet of plastic at least four feet (122 cm) wide, and a few rocks. [3] Next, find a place outside where you can dig a hole in the ground that will be one to two feet (30 to 60 cm) in diameter. [4] Dig the hole to a depth that is twice the height of the container. [5] Make sure that the bottom of the hole is flat. [6] Place the container in the center. [7] Place the sheet of plastic over the hole, and be careful not to knock dirt into the container. [8] Put a few rocks on the plastic to hold it in place. [9] In the center of the plastic, place a rock that is the size of an egg. [10] The weight of the rock will make a cone shape in the plastic above the container, but do not let the plastic touch the container. [11] Keep the plastic cone shape several inches above the container. [12] This shape will allow the drops of water that form on the plastic to run down into the cup. [13] Close the top of the hole by putting dirt around the edges of the plastic sheet. [14] If the top is not closed, the water will evaporate. [15] Leave the top closed overnight. [16] There should be some water in the container. [17] You can repeat this process until the hole is dry, at which time you can dig a new hole.

---

1. In sentence 3, add the adverb *approximately* to the size. Remember where to put an adverb when you use the verb *be*.

2. In sentence 4, the depth does not have to be exactly twice that of the container. Add the adverb *nearly* to the depth. Remember the rule with *be*.

3. At the beginning of sentence 7, the writer begins a new task. Add *Next* followed by a comma.

4. In sentence 7, add the adjective *any* before the word *dirt*.

5. In sentence 9, add the adverb *about* to the size.

6. In sentence 10, add the adverb *directly* in front of the phrase that begins with *above*. The writer needs to be very precise with the location.

7. Add the word *Finally* followed by a comma to the beginning of sentence 13 because this is the last step.

8. In sentence 14, add the adverb *tightly* to explain how it is closed.

9. In sentence 15, change the word *overnight* to a time phrase *until the next day*.

10. Sentence 16 needs a time. Add the clause *When you remove the cover* to the beginning of the sentence.

ACTIVITY 11   **Original Writing**

On a separate sheet of paper, write a paragraph (at least five sentences) that explains a process. Use at least one adverb of manner, one adverb of time, and one other adverb (frequency, degree, or certainty) and underline them.

Here are some examples of how to begin.

- *You can improve the quality of your digital photos with a few steps of a simple computer application.*
- *Many people enjoy looking at a beautiful painting without understanding how the artist created it. Here are a few things to look for that can help you analyze the process of a painting.*
- *You can grow fresh vegetables inexpensively by following these steps.*

APPENDIX 1 Building Greater Sentences

Being a good writer involves many skills, such as being able to write with correct grammar, vary your vocabulary, and state ideas concisely. A good writer also learns to create longer, more detailed sentences from simple ideas. Study the short sentences below.

> Jim Thorpe won two medals.
>
> The medals were Olympic medals.
>
> They were gold medals.
>
> He won them in 1912.
>
> He was not allowed to keep the medals.

Notice that every sentence has an important piece of information. A good writer would not write all these sentences separately. Instead, the most important information from each sentence can be used to create one longer, coherent sentence.

Read the sentences again; this time, the important information has been circled.

> Jim Thorpe won two medals.
>
> The medals were Olympic medals.
>
> They were gold medals.
>
> He won them in 1912.
>
> He was not allowed to keep the medals.

Here are some strategies for taking the circled information and creating a new sentence.

1. Create time phrases to introduce or end a sentence: in 1912
2. Find the key nouns: Jim Thorpe, medals
3. Find key adjectives: two, Olympic, gold
4. Create noun phrases: two + Olympic + gold + medals
5. Connect main ideas with conjunctions: but + not allowed to keep

Now read this improved, longer sentence:

> In 1912, Jim Thorpe won two Olympic gold medals, but was not allowed to keep them.

Here are some additional strategies for building better sentences.

1. Use coordinating conjunctions (*and, but, or, nor, yet, for, so*) to connect related ideas equally.
2. Use subordinating conjunctions, such as *after, while, since,* and *because* to connect related ideas when one idea is more important than the other.
3. Use clauses with relative pronouns, such as *who, which, that,* and *whose* to describe or define a noun or noun phrase.
4. Use pronouns to refer to previously mentioned information.

Part of Speech	Definition	Example
Adjective	An adjective is a word that describes a noun or pronoun.	Hurricane winds can be extremely **destructive**.
Adverb	An adverb is a word that describes a verb, an adjective, or another adverb.	Before starting any experiment, chemists must **carefully** prepare the chemicals involved.
Article	The definite article *the* is used with specific nouns. The indefinite articles *a* and *an* are used with singular count nouns.	**The** cottonmouth is **an** example of **a** poisonous snake.
Auxiliary	An auxiliary is a helping verb that is used with a main verb. Common auxiliaries are *be, do, have, will,* and modals such as *may, should,* and *could.*	Voters **did** not pass the new law, but supporters **may** try to write a different law.
Conjunction	A conjunction is used to connect words, phrases, or clauses. A coordinating conjunction connects two independent clauses. Common conjunctions are *and, but,* and *so.*	The capital of the United States used to be Philadelphia, **but** now it is Washington, D.C.
Noun	A noun is a person, place, thing, or idea. A noun can be used as an adjective.	The **Bengal tiger** has been listed as an endangered species since 2010.
Object	An object is a word that comes after a transitive (action) verb or a preposition.	Thomas Jefferson signed the **Declaration of Independence** in 1776.
Preposition	A preposition is a word that shows relationships between nouns, such as location, time, or direction. Prepositions can consist of one, two, or three words.	The books **about** gravity are located **in** the physics section **of** the library, **behind** the biology section.
Stative verb	Stative (nonactive) verbs describe states, senses, feelings, appearance, desires, or possession. Stative verbs are not usually used with progressive forms.	Early astronomers **believed** that Earth was the center of our universe.
Subject	The subject of a sentence tells who or what the sentence is about.	The **professor** is absent this term because he is on a sabbatical leave.
Verb	A verb shows the action of a sentence or the existence of something.	The people of Brazil **speak** Portuguese.

Basic Capitalization

Rule	Example
Always capitalize the first word of a sentence.	**T**oday the board members will meet to discuss the new zoning laws.
Always capitalize the word *I* no matter where it is in a sentence.	Although **I** have carefully planned, **I** realize that there are risks in the experiment.
Capitalize proper nouns—the names of specific people, places, or things. Capitalize a person's title, including *Mr.*, *Mrs.*, *Ms.*, and *Dr.*	**D**r. **S**mith teaches sociology with her colleague **M**s. Wong.
Capitalize names of countries and other geographic areas. Capitalize the names of people from those areas. Capitalize the names of languages.	The official language of **C**hina is **S**tandard **C**hinese, or **M**andarin. However, **C**hinese people speak many different language varieties and dialects.
Capitalize titles of works, such as books, movies, and pieces of art.	Art historians have been analyzing the ***Mona Lisa*** to learn about its history and the painting techniques used.

Geographic Names

Rule	Example
Use *the* with countries that look plural or have the word *United*, *Republic*, or *Kingdom.*	the Netherlands the Philippines the United States the United Kingdom the former Soviet Union the Kingdom of Saudi Arabia
Use *the* with deserts, forests, mountain ranges, and certain other geographic areas.	the Sahara Desert the Amazon Rain Forest the Middle East (*but* Southeast Asia) the Pacific Northwest the South
Use *the* with most bodies of water, except individual lakes.	the Nile River the Mississippi River the Atlantic Ocean the Mediterranean Sea the Great Lakes (*but* Lake Erie)

End Punctuation

Rule	Example
Period (.) A period is used at the end of a declarative sentence.	The Battle of Agincourt was fought in France in October of 1415**.**
Question mark (?) A question mark is used at the end of a question.	Which country gave the Statue of Liberty to the United States**?**
Exclamation point (!) An exclamation point is used at the end of an exclamation. It is very rarely used in academic writing.	The research team finally captured the giant squid on film**!**

Commas

Rule	Example
A comma separates the items in a list of three or more things. There should be a comma between each item in the list.	She speaks French**,** English**,** and Chinese.
A comma separates two independent clauses when there is a coordinating conjunction such as *and, but, or, so, for, nor,* and *yet*.	Students can register for classes in person**,** or they may submit their applications by mail.
A comma is used to separate an introductory word or phrase from the rest of the sentence.	In conclusion**,** doctors are advising people to make sure they exercise at least 20 minutes a day.
A comma is used to separate an appositive from the rest of the sentence. An appositive is a word or group of words that renames a noun before it and provides additional information about the noun.	Washington**,** <u>the first president of the United States</u>**,** was a clever military leader.
A comma is sometimes used with adjective clauses. An adjective clause usually begins with a relative pronoun (*who, that, which, whom, whose, whoever,* or *whomever*). Use a comma when the information in the clause is unnecessary or extra. (This is also called a nonrestrictive clause.)	*A Brief History of Time,* which was written by Steven Hawking, is an introduction to physics for readers new to the subject.

Base Form	Simple Past	Past Participle
be	was, were	been
beat	beat	beaten
become	became	become
begin	began	begun
bend	bent	bent
bite	bit	bitten
blow	blew	blown
break	broke	broken
bring	brought	brought
build	built	built
buy	bought	bought
catch	caught	caught
choose	chose	chosen
come	came	come
cost	cost	cost
cut	cut	cut
dig	dug	dug
dive	dived, dove	dived
do	did	done
draw	drew	drawn
drink	drank	drunk
drive	drove	driven
eat	ate	eaten
fall	fell	fallen
feed	fed	fed
feel	felt	felt
fight	fought	fought
find	found	found
fit	fit	fit, fitted
fly	flew	flown
forget	forgot	forgotten
forgive	forgave	forgiven
freeze	froze	frozen
get	got	got, gotten
give	gave	given
go	went	gone
grow	grew	grown
hang	hung	hung
have	had	had
hear	heard	heard
hide	hid	hidden
hit	hit	hit
hold	hid	hidden
hurt	hurt	hurt
keep	kept	kept
know	knew	known

Base Form	Simple Past	Past Participle
lay	laid	laid
light	lit, lighted	lit, lighted
lose	lost	lost
make	made	made
mean	meant	meant
meet	met	met
pay	paid	paid
prove	proved	proved, proven
put	put	put
quit	quit	quit
read	read	read
ride	rode	ridden
ring	rang	rung
rise	rose	risen
run	ran	run
say	said	said
seek	sought	sought
sit	sat	sat
sleep	slept	slept
slide	slid	slid
speak	spoke	spoken
spend	spent	spent
spread	spread	spread
stand	stood	stood
steal	stole	stolen
stick	stuck	stuck
strike	struck	struck
swear	swore	sworn
sweep	swept	swept
swim	swam	swum
take	took	taken
teach	taught	taught
tear	tore	torn
tell	told	told
think	thought	thought
throw	threw	thrown
understand	understood	understood
upset	upset	upset
wake	woke	woken
wear	wore	worn
win	won	won
write	wrote	written

APPENDIX 5 Prepositions

Prepositions

Single			Multi-word
about	between	onto	according to
above	beyond	opposite	because of
across	by	out	due to
against	down	outside	in back/front of
along	during	over	in place of
among	for	since	in spite of
around	from	through	instead of
as	in	throughout	next to
at	inside	toward(s)	with regard to
before	into	underneath	
behind	near	until	
below	of	up	
beneath	off	upon	
beside	on	with	
		within	
		without	

Preposition Combinations

Verb + Preposition

account for	differ from	look for/at	talk about
agree with	focus on	participate in	wait for
depend on	listen to	result in	worry about

Adjective + Preposition

afraid of	consistent with	interested in	similar to
associated with	different from	necessary for	tired of
aware of	familiar with	ready for	worried about
capable of	famous for	related to	
compared to/with	important for	satisfied with	

Noun + Preposition

the cause of	the example of	the need for	the reason for
the development of	the increase in	the number of	the relationship between
the difference between	the lack of	the percent of	

Sentence Fragments

Definition	Solution
A sentence fragment is a group of words that is not a complete sentence. A fragment is usually missing either a subject or a verb, or it is a dependent clause. A dependent clause is never a complete sentence. To correct a sentence fragment: • add a subject or verb, *or* • combine two clauses	**Add a subject.** ✗ A fungus is not an animal. Is an organism belonging to a group called *Fungi*. ✓ A fungus is not an animal. **It** is an organism belonging to a group called *Fungi*. **Combine two clauses.** ✗ Charles Darwin traveled to the Galapagos Islands. Because he wanted to study the unique creatures. ✓ Charles Darwin traveled to the Galapagos Islands **because** he wanted to study the unique creatures.

Run-on Sentences

Definition	Solution
A run-on sentence is two sentences incorrectly joined without a comma and coordinating conjunction (*and, but,* or *so*). To correct a run-on sentence: • add a comma and a connecting word, *or* • add a period to separate the sentence into two sentences	**Separate into two sentences.** ✗ The three branches of the United States government are the Executive, the Legislative, and the Judicial branches the president is part of the Executive branch. ✓ The three branches of the United States government are the Executive, the Legislative, and the Judicial branches**. T**he president is part of the Executive branch.

Comma Splices

Definition	Solution
A comma splice occurs when two or more sentences or independent clauses are connected with a comma. To correct a comma splice: • add a connecting word after the comma, • create two sentences from the one, *or* • combine the most important words into one sentence and add a subordinating conjunction (*because, since, although*)	**Add a connecting word.** ✗ Michelangelo created his statue *David* in 1504, it is considered a masterpiece of Renaissance sculpture. ✓ Michelangelo created his statue *David* in 1504, **and** it is considered a masterpiece of Renaissance sculpture. **Create two sentences.** ✓ Michelangelo created his statue *David* in 1504**. It** is considered a masterpiece of Renaissance sculpture. **Add a subordinating conjunction.** ✗ Astronauts usually stay on the International Space Station for only four to six months, being in zero gravity is hard on the human body. ✓ **Because** being in zero gravity is hard on the human body, astronauts usually stay on the International Space Station for only four to six months.

A paragraph is a group of sentences about one topic or one idea. It may have a title at the top. The first sentence of the paragraph is indented. The topic sentence is usually near the beginning and introduces the main idea. The sentences in the body of the paragraph are connected to the topic sentence. They support and build on the main idea with facts, details, and reasons. The concluding sentence usually states the main point again or summarizes the main idea of the paragraph.

The Effect of Cellphones on Drivers — Title

A recent study by Donald Redelmeir and Rovert Tibshirani of the University of Toronto showed that cellular phones pose a risk to drivers. — Indented first line / Topic sentence

In fact, people who talk on the phone while driving are four times more likely to have an automobile accident than those who do not use the phone while driving. The Toronto researchers studied 699 drivers who had been in an automobile accident while they were using their cellular phones. The researchers concluded that the main reason for the accidents was not that people used one hand for the telephone and had one hand on the steering wheel. Rather the cause of the accidents was usually that the drivers became distracted, angry, or upset by the phone call. The drivers then lost concentration and were more likely to be in a car accident. — Body of paragraph with supporting sentences

The study showed why using cellular phones while driving leads to increased accidents. — Concluding sentence

Averil Coxhead (2000)

The following words are on the Academic Word List (AWL). The AWL is a list of the 570 highest-frequency academic word families that regularly appear in academic texts. The AWL was compiled by researcher Averil Coxhead based on her analysis of a 3.5-million-word corpus of academic texts and is reprinted with her permission.

abandon	assign	commit	contribute
abstract	assist	commodity	controversy
academy	assume	communicate	convene
access	assure	community	converse
accommodate	attach	compatible	convert
accompany	attain	compensate	convince
accumulate	attitude	compile	cooperate
accurate	attribute	complement	coordinate
achieve	author	complex	core
acknowledge	authority	component	corporate
acquire	automate	compound	correspond
adapt	available	comprehensive	couple
adequate	aware	comprise	create
adjacent	behalf	compute	credit
adjust	benefit	conceive	criteria
administrate	bias	concentrate	crucial
adult	bond	concept	culture
advocate	brief	conclude	currency
affect	bulk	concurrent	cycle
aggregate	capable	conduct	data
aid	capacity	confer	debate
albeit	category	confine	decade
allocate	cease	confirm	decline
alter	challenge	conflict	deduce
alternative	channel	conform	define
ambiguous	chapter	consent	definite
amend	chart	consequent	demonstrate
analogy	chemical	considerable	denote
analyze	circumstance	consist	deny
annual	cite	constant	depress
anticipate	civil	constitute	derive
apparent	clarify	constrain	design
append	classic	construct	despite
appreciate	clause	consult	detect
approach	code	consume	deviate
appropriate	coherent	contact	device
approximate	coincide	contemporary	devote
arbitrary	collapse	context	differentiate
area	colleague	contract	dimension
aspect	commence	contradict	diminish
assemble	comment	contrary	discrete
assess	commission	contrast	discriminate

displace	exploit	imply	layer
display	export	impose	lecture
dispose	expose	incentive	legal
distinct	external	incidence	legislate
distort	extract	incline	levy
distribute	facilitate	income	liberal
diverse	factor	incorporate	license
document	feature	index	likewise
domain	federal	indicate	link
domestic	fee	individual	locate
dominate	file	induce	logic
draft	final	inevitable	maintain
drama	finance	infer	major
duration	finite	infrastructure	manipulate
dynamic	flexible	inherent	manual
economy	fluctuate	inhibit	margin
edit	focus	initial	mature
element	format	initiate	maximize
eliminate	formula	injure	mechanism
emerge	forthcoming	innovate	media
emphasis	found	input	mediate
empirical	foundation	insert	medical
enable	framework	insight	medium
encounter	function	inspect	mental
energy	fund	instance	method
enforce	fundamental	institute	migrate
enhance	furthermore	instruct	military
enormous	gender	integral	minimal
ensure	generate	integrate	minimize
entity	generation	integrity	minimum
environment	globe	intelligent	ministry
equate	goal	intense	minor
equip	grade	interact	mode
equivalent	grant	intermediate	modify
erode	guarantee	internal	monitor
error	guideline	interpret	motive
establish	hence	interval	mutual
estate	hierarchy	intervene	negate
estimate	highlight	intrinsic	network
ethic	hypothesis	invest	neutral
ethnic	identical	investigate	nevertheless
evaluate	identify	invoke	nonetheless
eventual	ideology	involve	norm
evident	ignorant	isolate	normal
evolve	illustrate	issue	notion
exceed	image	item	notwithstanding
exclude	immigrate	job	nuclear
exhibit	impact	journal	objective
expand	implement	justify	obtain
expert	implicate	label	obvious
explicit	implicit	labor	occupy

occur
odd
offset
ongoing
option
orient
outcome
output
overall
overlap
overseas
panel
paradigm
paragraph
parallel
parameter
participate
partner
passive
perceive
percent
period
persist
perspective
phase
phenomenon
philosophy
physical
plus
policy
portion
pose
positive
potential
practitioner
precede
precise
predict
predominant
preliminary
presume
previous
primary
prime
principal
principle
prior
priority
proceed
process
professional

prohibit
project
promote
proportion
prospect
protocol
psychology
publication
publish
purchase
pursue
qualitative
quote
radical
random
range
ratio
rational
react
recover
refine
regime
region
register
regulate
reinforce
reject
relax
release
relevant
reluctance
rely
remove
require
research
reside
resolve
resource
respond
restore
restrain
restrict
retain
reveal
revenue
reverse
revise
revolution
rigid
role

route
scenario
schedule
scheme
scope
section
sector
secure
seek
select
sequence
series
sex
shift
significant
similar
simulate
site
so-called
sole
somewhat
source
specific
specify
sphere
stable
statistic
status
straightforward
strategy
stress
structure
style
submit
subordinate
subsequent
subsidy
substitute
successor
sufficient
sum
summary
supplement
survey
survive
suspend
sustain
symbol
tape
target

task
team
technical
technique
technology
temporary
tense
terminate
text
theme
theory
thereby
thesis
topic
trace
tradition
transfer
transform
transit
transmit
transport
trend
trigger
ultimate
undergo
underlie
undertake
uniform
unify
unique
utilize
valid
vary
vehicle
version
via
violate
virtual
visible
vision
visual
volume
voluntary
welfare
whereas
whereby
widespread